KU-755-629

# THE NEW 'GRAND TOUR'

Travelling today through Europe, Asia Minor, India and Nepal

by

FREDERICK ALDERSON

# DAVID & CHARLES

NEWTON ABBOT

ISBN 0 7153 5005 6

COPYRIGHT NOTICE

© Frederick Alderson 1971

All rights reserved. No part of this
publication may be reproduced, stored
in a retrieval system, or transmitted,
in any form or by any means, electronic,
mechanical, photocopying, recording or
otherwise, without the prior permission
of David & Charles (Publishers) Limited

Set in 11pt Baskerville 2pt leaded
and printed in Great Britain
by Bristol Typesetting Company Limited
for David & Charles (Publishers) Limited
South Devon House Newton Abbot Devon

# CONTENTS

To the Sundowners

# LIST OF ILLUSTRATIONS

(*The photographs not otherwise acknowledged were taken by the author.*)

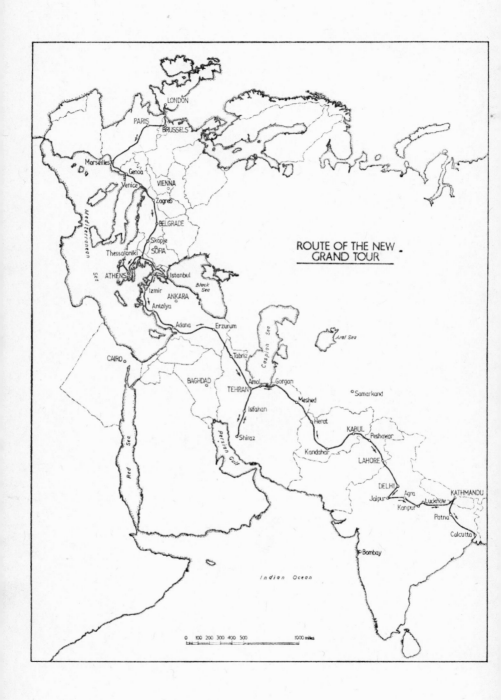

ROUTE OF THE NEW
GRAND TOUR

# 1 GRAND TOURISM

*The cavalcade set out on the road to Dover. As the commodore could not bear the fatigue of jolting they travelled at an easy pace during the first stage, so that the old gentleman had an opportunity of communicating his exhortations to his godson, with regard to his conduct abroad: he advised him, now that he was going into foreign parts, to be on his guard against the fair weather of French politesse, which was no more to be trusted than a whirlpool at sea. He observed that many young men had gone to Paris with good cargoes of sense, and returned with a great deal of canvass, and no ballast at all, whereby they became crank all the days of their lives, and sometimes carried their keels above water. He desired Mr Jolter to keep his pupil out of the clutches of those sharking priests who lie in wait to make converts of all young strangers, and in a particular manner cautioned the youth against carnal conversation with Parisian dames, who, he understood, were no better than gaudy fireships ready primed with death and destruction.*

With thanks for the one-eyed commodore's kind admonitions, with a hundred guineas in his pocket from his aunt, with Jolter, his travelling 'governor', and a lacquey and Swiss valet who had already made the tour of Europe, astride their horses, Peregrine Pickle thus set out for France and the Low Countries in the manner expected of a young mid-eighteenth century gentleman. His subsequent adventures and discoveries, from an affray with Customs at Calais and a short 'cooler' in the Bastille, to return by packet from Rotterdam, and his round of sights from

the Palais Royal and Luxembourg gallery to the Leyden physics-
garden and anatomical hall, are recounted by Smollett in a
manner calculated to send up the image of the young Englishman abroad, while not neglecting to knock the pretensions of
foreigners. But what were the real merits and expected results of
the Grand Tour?

One of the benefits to the Englishman of being born insular
is the extra inducement to him to travel. Those with frontiers
linking country with country in uninterrupted series from, say,
Italy to India, are not as subject to the urge as those cut off from
all other countries by sea. Although commonly regarded as an
eighteenth-century habit, the Grand Tour had in fact come in
along with heightened national consciousness under Queen
Elizabeth I. She, by Royal Bounty, ensured that 'young men of
whom good hopes were conceived' could set forth 'into several
parts beyond the seas', as a crown of their education, to be
trained and made fit for public employment and to learn the
languages. The amount need not be much : they travelled as
private gentlemen and had their reward in employment or prefer-
ment afterwards. Philip Sidney is one of the noteworthy
examples. Sometimes an allowance of £20 a year might come
from a college, since 'in the younger sort,' as Bacon puts it, 'travel
is a part of education'. Fynes Moryson, Fellow of Peterhouse,
Cambridge, enjoyed that provision in 1591, as did the present
writer in his day.

Within a generation the diarist Evelyn was embarking on
much the same round as tourists were to follow for a couple of
hundred years : first Holland and Belgium, then France, Italy
as far as Rome, Naples and Venice, then back via Switzerland.
His expenses, including personal servants and fees to guides,
boatmen and soldier-guards where needed, averaged about £300
a year for his four years of travel, but this covered considerable
outlay on pictures and antiquities. Evelyn was also one of the
earliest tourists to 'take a landscape' or sketch of notable
scenes.

By the end of the seventeenth century 'Spectator' Addison,
who had been given a state pension to allow him to 'cultivate

his classic tastes by travel on the Continent', was not only doing the French and Italian 'giro', including Vienna, the Tirol and parts of Germany, but had been offered expenses and a fee of a hundred guineas a year to act as travelling tutor to a nobleman.

After the victories of Queen Anne's reign, the period of comparative peace abroad that obtained during most of the reigns of George I and George II (despite the Seven Years' War) and Britain's growing prosperity under Walpole's administration, greatly favoured Grand Tourism. Its popularity then has led to its identification with that age of taste and culture and in fact the tour's object was often to acquire some, if only of the social chit-chat sort. Young Englishmen of wealth and family, eldest sons in particular, were sent off for a year or two's travel with a tutor or 'bear-leader' to get a little more polish, width of interest and outlook before they settled down to the routine of fox-hunt, claret, bench or pocket borough and their inheritance. If only new fashions and new forms of dissipation rubbed off on the wilder spirits, and they spent their allowance running after women and bad company, others made acquaintance with the manners of courts, with savants of European reputation and with styles of art and architecture that would fructify when they came into their own at home.

To take the latter first. The great landed nobles, the country gentry and rich merchants, and to some extent also the comfortable middle classes, were able to build and adorn their palaces and country houses in the prosperous peaceful years of the early eighteenth century. There was an efflorescence in architecture and in the English school of painting for which travel abroad either by patron or artist or both did much to provide stimulus. Sometimes results were patently due to inspirations found on tour. Lord Burlington, for example, having come of age and succeeded to his estates in Yorkshire and southern Ireland, made the tour of Italy in 1715: there he became so enamoured of Palladian architecture that he founded a school of architects to design buildings in that style. The improvements of Burlington House were one result. Chiswick House, in whose building Burl-

ington the amateur was associated with William Kent the professional, another, Kent also having spent some years in Rome
and Venice. Chiswick was based on a design adapted from
Palladio's Villa Rotonda at Vicenza and was intended not as a
residence, but to house his lordship's art collection. It has one of
the first copies of a Roman ceiling. Again, the frescoed staircase
at Kensington Palace reveals Kent as not far inferior to the
Italians themselves.

Not a few of these grand tourists wrote and published accounts
of their travels, sometimes illustrated by topographic artists whom
they had taken in their train. This in turn provided a means of
developing the talents of our early landscape painters, such as
Richard Wilson (1714-82) and J. R. Cozens (1752-97). The
Dilettanti Society was formed by fifty peers and peers' sons who
had been on the Grand Tour, with the object of helping promis-
ing artists to travel abroad. Stubbs and Allan Ramsay were
among those who profited. After the rediscovery of Pompeii noble
connoisseurs were more attracted to classical art; Lord Charle-
mont, on his travels to Italy and Greece, had engravings by
Piranesi dedicated to him. A further benefit conferred by the
Dilettanti was the princely patronage given to the publication of
volumes on Ionian antiquities after an expedition to Asia Minor
early in George III's reign.

Apart from this encouragement to artists and the embellish-
ment of stately homes with their works, the golden years of the
Grand Tour had other desirable effects on our insularity. In
what came to be regarded as the traditional round, the English
gentleman was led through a succession of German courts, down
to the principal cities of Italy, then back through France from
Montpellier to Paris. Men and manners were the primary interest. From the great houses of England he was linked by introductions to château, schloss and palazzo, where the degree of his
ease of address and ability to shake off national prejudices was
almost a barometer for the enjoyment of hospitality. Not all, like
Peregrine Pickle, shocked foreigners by ostentatious English pre-
ferences abroad or, on their return home, assumed foreign
manners and contempt for any others. The squire born a Lump-

kin was no doubt destined to be always a Lumpkin, albeit a bolder one, and to justify the quip

> How much a dunce, that has been sent to roam,
> Excels a dunce that has been kept at home.

But there were others, such as James Boswell. It is summer 1763 : 'I am now,' he writes to a friend, 'a young man of fortune just going to set out on his travels. That time which I have often looked forward to is arrived. My father [Lord Auchinleck] wants to have me go as soon as possible. . . . I am in charming spirits. Would that I could make the tour of Europe in such a frame.' It is arranged that he will go first to Germany with Lord Marischal, a Scottish nobleman as familiar with German courts as Boswell is with the houses of other Ayrshire lairds; his father, pleased at the idea, gives him a 'genteel credit' of £30 per month. While abroad he intends to lay up a store of pleasing ideas and on his return home become a useful member of society.

Next summer, after a short circuit of Holland, with a chance-met American traveller, John Morgan, they are off. Boswell travels to Brunswick and is presented at court; to Potsdam where he views the king's palace and Sanssouci; to Berlin, lodging there with the president of the city council and conversing with the British envoy, who had accompanied Frederick the Great on his campaigns during the Seven Years' War. After that he is anxious to spend some months in Italy and enlists both the envoy's and Lord Marischal's aid to break down his father's opposition to that 'intoxicating region'. Meanwhile, with his trunks in the post waggon he tours to Dessau, where he is received at court and taken stag-hunting; to Leipzig, in the bustle of fair time, but he sees the 'learned city's two noble Library's and elegant gardens'; to Dresden, 'most beautiful city that I ever saw'; then to Saxe-Gotha, home of George III's mother, and Mannheim, where the Elector Palatine gives operas and comedies and concerts, but fails to invite him to dine, so that he is obliged to eat at an 'ordinary' among fellows 'of all sorts and sizes', which disgusts him; and to meet Voltaire and Rousseau—as Addison had met and conversed with Boileau in Paris. He does so and believes that Rousseau's conversation will have an influence on the whole of his future existence—Voltaire's will merely add rich foreign treasure to his 'papers'.

After Switzerland, where he finds a swarm of British, Boswell gets his wish and under the protection of the Dominican Friars, with letters of recommendation from convent to convent, he goes from Turin to Milan, Parma and Bologna, thence to Rome, Florence, Naples and finally Venice. Turin disappoints: it lacks elegance and manners and contains a great number of idle men and abandoned women, who spend their time in 'gross gallantry' and 'coupled without sentiment'. But of the other Italian cities —many of which are known generally 'only by the back or belly', ie by their specialities in food, drink and fabrics: Genoese velvet, Parmesan cheese, Venetian poplins etc—he writes enthusiastically, especially when he can view the very scenes celebrated by such classical poets as Horace or Virgil.

After two weeks in Venice, 'the most curious town in the world', now in the company of Lord Mountstuart and his governor and travelling tutor, Boswell makes his return, although not before both young men have taken up with the same opera dancer—blaming of course the Italian climate for 'inflaming hot desires'—and contracted pox. He travels back via Parma and Florence, jaunts through the rest of Tuscany, then sails from Leghorn via Corsica to Genoa, 'truly what Mr Addison made me expect' and embarks for France.

Although his father expects him home before winter, Boswell dallies in the 'country of gayety' well into January. He attends a religious procession in Nice, takes a brief look at Monaco, views the naval anchorage (but is not allowed into the arsenal) at Toulon, admires the theatre and free manners of the people of Marseilles, which he considers one of the prettiest towns in France, visits Aix and Avignon cathedrals and the Roman remains at Nîmes then, reluctantly, after a diversion to the health resort of Montpellier and a few days at Lyons, where frost and sore toes keep him indoors, he takes the diligence for Paris. He has been away from his twenty-fourth to his twenty-sixth year,

Page 17: (*left*) In the square at Eleutherou-polis; (*right*) Eleutherou-polis, Macedonia

Page 18: (*left*) Acropolis from the Agora, Athens; (*right*) Tholos, Delphi

a period of over sixteen months. Without claiming to be a virtuoso, he feels now that he has formed a lifelong taste for the arts and determines to continue his study with the help of books and prints in his father's library. He has stored his memory with rich ideas and in the courts he declares he has had the most advantageous opportunity of forming his manners. Altogether then Boswell, an unusually self-conscious (though bumptious) member of the Age of Privilege, regards himself as one of the most fortunate young men alive and hopes to show when he has 'put on the gown' as advocate that he is grateful. 'Who knows but I may yet rejoice my father's heart?'

Boswell's mode of travel, unlike that of some English gentlemen who travelled with their servants, horses and dogs and never minded money, is economical wherever possible. In Germany he uses the post waggon, a large cart on high wheels with no covering and only deal boards for seats, 'a hurdle called a post chaise', as another contemporary terms it, or else the equally uncomfortable closed waggon. He sleeps on the straw-strewn commonroom floors of inns, until the iron stove makes the air so foul that he seeks a hay loft in the cold. In Italy he sometimes starts out at three in the morning; in France both leaves and arrives in the dark, since the diligence starts at four or five in the morning. For the diligence, the cheapest way of travel, he has nothing but praise, compared with either the post waggon or the English stagecoach. It costs 100 livres for 100 leagues, all found, and although cumbrous is roomy inside and in the cabriolet outside offers chance to enjoy the passing scene while shielded from sun and rain. The conductor or coachman, a person of great consequence, negotiates all meals at inns and receives the traveller's complaints. Even after another sixty years the French diligence remains far superior to the cramped, low-roofed and airless German type.

Dr Johnson, whose great regret was his unsatisfied passion for travel, opined that 'A man who has not been in Italy is always conscious of an inferiority'. The writers of the age seized the chance to fill this gap for others, at any rate vicariously. Smollett and Sterne, Goldsmith and Gray, Mrs Piozzi and Mrs Radcliffe

B

all made the tour—Goldsmith on foot—and reported it, with
satire or sentiment, poetry or picturesque extravagance or philo-
sophising, in their individual fashion. (Mrs Piozzi made the most
unusual 'extra', with her dog, from Vienna to Prague.) By the
last decade of the century a less well-known tourist, James Smith,
could list a score of general works in English relating to the tour
of France and Italy, beginning with Addison and ending with
Arthur Young, but excluding professed and detailed guides* like
the *Grand Tour* published in 1749 by Dr Thomas Nugent.

The poet Thomas Gray introduced a different note into tourist
literature, finding on his visit in 1741 to the monastery of Grande
Chartreuse, which he reached up the mountain on mule-back,
every precipice, torrent and cliff 'pregnant with religion and
poetry'. Most travellers, like Boswell, regarded mountains as a
necessary stage, as in crossing the Mont Cenis to Italy, not as an
object of a journey : whenever possible they cut them out altogether by using the sea route to or from Marseilles. (If a gentleman chose to use his own carriage on tour it had to be a vehicle
that would take to pieces, whether for crossing the Alps or avoiding them.) But after Gray and popular works on landscape by the
naturalist Thomas Pennant, visitors to the Grande Chartreuse
were out to see not merely the treasures of the monastery, but its
picturesque and romantic approach : cascades speeding down
precipices into foaming gulfs far below, mountains shaggy with
hanging woods and snows above—in fact the genius of the place
itself. When Mrs Radcliffe came to write her best-sellers, such as
*The Mysteries of Udolpho*, she could incorporate into their atmosphere of terror, landscape descriptions of extravagance and
gloom with sure-fire effect.

Some idea of the tourist traffic during this century can be
obtained from the contemporary estimate that in the two years
immediately following the Seven Years' War, forty thousand
English people passed through the customs at Calais. Laurence
Sterne was one of them. In wartime, governments then were not
so severe on non-combatants of even an enemy nation, but the

---

* Such early guides gave maps of post-routes, rate of exchange, distances
and names of hotels.

painter Hogarth had been arrested at Calais previously, which was inconvenient, and a fellow artist had been imprisoned for a time in the Bastille. Before the outbreak of the Napoleonic wars, which forced tourists either north to Germany or south into Spain—of the two thousand who rushed to Paris during the short abortive Peace of Amiens one thousand English were kept interned at Verdun until the war ended eleven years later—one of the last travellers to publish his account was James Edward Smith, MD FRS. His *Sketch of a Tour on the Continent* appeared in the fatal year 1793.

Dr Smith's claims to interest in a field which, as he says, has already afforded so many rich harvests (though some rather carelessly gathered) are his observations on natural history. 'The travelling observer of nature has, as it were, the enjoyment of a new sense in addition to those common to the rest of mankind. He can find amusement and instruction where they bemoan themselves as in a wilderness.' He therefore plans to avoid the travelling herd and mix as much as possible with the people of each country, especially the literary and scientific. So while not omitting the usual description of pictures, buildings, men and manners in Holland, France and Italy, nor in the course of it failing to correct those predecessors whose travel notes he had read up beforehand, this young man offers another way of profiting from the Grand Tour at a time when 'the changes in French affairs are so rapid, the decisions so violent and unexpected that imagination cannot keep pace with them'. To what degree the monuments at St Denis and at Paris, the curiosities at Chantilly and other things have suffered is not exactly known in England, but 'the tame carp at Chantilly were destroyed very early in the revolution'.

After having his baggage examined at Valenciennes 'with all that troublesome exactness and that insolence of office, so unpleasant to an honest man and yet so insufficient to prevent fraud', Smith takes the usual route: Paris ('an hotel where gilt tables and silk furniture but ill atoned for the dirty brick floors'), Chantilly, Lyons, Montpellier, Nîmes, Marseilles. . . . Versailles offers him a sight of the royal family going in to chapel, but its

general magnificence cuts less ice with him than its lake, which
produces abundant water caltrops, a plant whose fruit is edible
and tastes like chestnut; this, he thinks, might be naturalised in
our marshland ditches. Rousseau is dead now, but he visits the
savant's widow at the place of his retirement near the forest of
Chantilly, examines a collection of his dried plants pasted on
writing paper with their Linnaean names and is able to enter the
hut 'commanding a delicious landscape', where Rousseau sat and
contemplated nature. Botany was Rousseau's last consolation
and the traveller is thrilled to find among the rocks near the hut
a lichen which he has never found elsewhere. He has, of course,
already visited the botanic gardens in Leyden, Amsterdam and
Paris to compare their contents with Kew and meet their
curators, and will later seek out that at Montpellier founded in
Henry IV's time. But his liveliest observations are of the wayside
shrubs and flowers which characterise the approaches to various
towns.

Towards Avignon there is a profusion of box, thyme and
lavender, at Marseilles honey-scented alyssum (in the market a
fine show of spring flowers including carnations), near Toulon
rosemary, juniper and erica : one looks to see how many such
wild gardens exist today. Just beyond Marseilles there is the usual
customs fuss, another strict examination 'at that formidable
bureau mentioned by Smollett' and he is fairly launched upon the
Riviera, then only lately discovered as a British resort. He sees
his first date palm in open ground near Hyères, myrtles grow on
the slopes and American aloe (*Agave Americana*) in immense
tufts among the rocks; near Cannes there are cistus and arbutus
and great ten foot shrubs of tree heath. Nice is cold for mid-
December with ice on the roads, and 'the galley-slaves chained
two together walking about the streets are not an agreeable
spectacle to a humane mind', but rosemary is in flower and again
there are delightful roadside shrubberies of aloe, myrtle and
heathers. Monaco has precipices below the town covered with the
Indian fig, whose leaves when pulped relieve gout, and leadwort
and navelwort among the rocks. Near his inn he finds an arum
in flower 'which the inhabitants call *il lume* (the lamp) from the

striking resemblance of its flower, when reversed, to a lamp with its wick'. (It is an interesting topic, touched on by Sir Edward Salisbury, late director of the Royal Botanic Gardens, Kew, to conjecture which of our 'weeds and aliens', now seemingly established as native, were brought back from the Grand Tour, either intentionally or perhaps in the packing of statuary and other objets d'art, by accident.)

Here, then, we may leave Dr Smith to sail to St Remo and then, as the wind turned east and made the felucca impracticable, to venture by land with a guide and mules, only a little money but 'two very good pistols for banditti', along 'that formidable road, the corniche to Genoa', among groves of olive and carob trees and then, later, fields with borders of Carthusian pinks in flower and saffron butterflies.

While the main approach to the Continent was closed by war, Byron's urge to travel impelled him to seek regions of Europe which few tourists could afford: Spain, Greece, Constantinople. After the wars were over the aristocratic style of Grand Tour underwent a change, the old idea of it as a training ground for England's future rulers merging into that of a romantic and picturesque extended vacation. The plebeian and the pilgrim were more in evidence than the nobleman and his tutor. When Hazlitt, for example, crossed from Brighton to Dieppe, on his journey the passengers were not scions of the aristocracy, but younger sons of wealthy citizens just finished at university. Instead of Milor Anglais there were pilgrim poets, following the example on foot of Shelley, and pilgrim painters, hoping to make money out of the tour by contributing material for steel engravings in the Landscape Annuals, Keepsakes and Books of Beauty, published by Ackermann and others, which were the coffee-table books of the day. Samuel Rogers' *Italy* carried illustrations by Turner and Stothard when its second edition appeared in 1830. The Gothic is more to their taste than the classical, the proximity of the picturesque compensates for the pedestrian's lack of comfort. An Albert Smith is content to travel through France and the Alps to Milan, in 1838, on foot with only £12 sterling for five weeks.

Byron's tour is of a different order, both in manner and results.

After contemplating a voyage to the East 'costing not more than £500' (but carrying £3,000 with him in case of emergency), he finally left in July 1809 by the Falmouth packet for Lisbon with his friend Hobhouse and over £100 worth of books. They swam the Tagus, frolicked in Seville, then proceeded via Gibraltar, Sardinia and Malta to Albania—dressing the part in romantic Albanian costume at fifty guineas each—and Athens, where Byron was appalled by Lord Elgin's recent despoliation of the Acropolis. (He presented the municipality with an iron clock in lieu of the Parthenon frieze.) From Athens they went on to Smyrna and Troy: Byron swam the Hellespont, like Leander, from Sestos to Abydos; then to Constantinople. When he came back to Falmouth, two years after leaving, Byron had *Childe Harold's Pilgrimage* in his pocket and hatred for Turkish cruelty, filth and dominion in his heart. 'If I am poet,' he wrote, 'the air of Greece has made me one.' Subsequently the air of Greece was to replace that of Rome as the ideal spiritual and intellectual climate for Europeans.

Five years later Byron set out on his second tour, leaving England for ever, and with the second part of *Childe Harold* provided the manual for a whole generation of tourists less sophisticated than himself. This time, in a specially built travelling coach, with its library, plate chest and every apparatus for dining—the sort of vehicle that had store cellars under seats, secret drawers under windows, pockets in the lining, spring blinds, fitted non-slip cushions and comfortable rounded corners—he rode to Ghent, Antwerp, Brussels, Cologne, Lausanne, Geneva and, after meeting Shelley in Switzerland, to Milan, Venice ('the greenest island of my imagination'), and then Rome and Ravenna. The landscapes that Byron had seen, transfused with history and described as no one had described them before, inspired most subsequent travellers. When Edward and William Finden's illustrations to Byron's works came out, with their beautiful engravings by Turner and other artists and their notes of local colour, the effect was well-nigh irresistible.

Wherever he went Byron made places memorable or left them with a legend—as when in Venice he swam a race with an ex-

soldier of Napoleon from the Lido to the Grand Canal, being
over four hours in the water and beating him by five hundred
yards or, according to tradition, after a late carouse would throw
himself into the canal fully dressed and then strike out for his
palazzo, swimming with one hand and holding up a lantern to
warn passing gondoliers with the other!

As Byron remarked to Hobhouse, 'it has been our fortune to
traverse together the countries of chivalry, history and fable—
Spain, Greece, Asia Minor and Italy', and in double sense it was
a matter of fortune. Within twenty years, however, while middle
class families were venturing to Switzerland and Italy, Edward
Lear was beginning a more ambitious series of journeys, first to
Italy, then to Sicily,* Albania, Corfu, Greece, Constantinople
and Palestine. The going was not plushy: the dirt in the village
inns of the Abruzzi and the weariness of five whole days, from
three or four in a morning till five at night, in a vetturino, with
rumours of cholera and highway robbers, on the way from
Florence to Rome, struck him forcibly. But he toured about
Lugano and Como and Naples on foot, covered the whole Greek
peninsula from Salonika to Sunium and was busy with sketch-
book and pencil wherever he went. The result was *Illustrated
Excursions in Italy* dealing with the Abruzzi provinces and the
Papal States, and *Journal of a Landscape Painter in Greece and
Albania* (1851), a lively account of regions which even today are
comparatively little known to us. (Cf the London *Observer Re-
view*, January 1970 : 'some write off Albania as a primitive, lawless, brigand-haunted region.')

Lear's ultimate ambition was to illustrate the scenery of all
the countries of southern Europe and the Near East and then to
seek escape from insular monotony further east. Before the
decade was over he had been as far as Jerusalem and Petra,
where he showed considerable coolness, when surrounded by two
hundred fellaheen in the great cliff-hung valley with its one long
tortuous cleft of exit and approach, refusing to fire his five-

* Sicily up to this time had attracted few tourists owing to lack of roads
and tolerable inns, although John Ray, pioneer botanist, had been there
two hundred years earlier.

barrelled revolver, 'which would have been the signal for our
instant sacrifice', even when the mob of shrieking Arabs pulled
him about and rifled his pockets of everything they held, 'from
dollars and penknives to handkerchiefs and hard-boiled eggs'. He
found his drawing on these forays both a benefit and a draw-
back : sometimes he could effect communication by it with
suspicious strangers, at other times he was liable to be stoned, as
in the towns of remote Albania, under Turkish dominion and
Mohammedan by religion, as one 'sent by the Sultan to write us
all down before he sells us to the Russian Emperor'. It was even
worse there than in India, where he was able to go on his last
tour with commissions to paint the scene for the new viceroy.

Meanwhile the European scene had had Ruskin's eye upon
it (from his travelling carriage) : thereafter tourists who had seen
what Byron saw were succeeded by those who saw what Ruskin
saw, with all that meant in the way of natural and artistic appre-
ciation. By the 1850s, the expert advice of Baedeker's and Murray's guides, the advent of Bradshaw and Thomas Cook,* the
steamer service on the Rhine and the continental railway develop-
ment which within a few years brought Rome to within sixty
hours of London, were already superannuating the carriage and
courier mode of travel. (The rapid growth of the railways and
consequent cut in travel time brought touring within reach of
middle range incomes and leisure, permitting to Englishmen
more regular continental trips instead of the once-for-all prolonged tour.)

Nevertheless Dickens, Augustus Egg, RA and Wilkie Collins
adopted the old route, more or less, and the old way when they
set out on their own abbreviated version of the Grand Tour in
1853. Travelling in a weird variety of vehicles, 'like swings, like
boats, like Noah's Arks, like barges and enormous bedsteads',
they posted to Lausanne, after rail from Paris to Basle, made an
excursion to Chillon, (made famous by Byron's poem *The
Prisoner of Chillon*) and to Chamonix, to ascend the Mer de
Glace, by that time as essential a tourist sight as sunset on Mont

* Cook conducted in person his first 'Great Circular Tour of the Continent' in 1856; Murray's handbooks began in 1836, Baedeker's in 1839.

Blanc. Then, at the rate of 12-75 miles per day, they crossed Switzerland to Milan (hearing the latest Verdi opera at La Scala), and Genoa. P & O steamship took them on to Naples (for Pompeii and ascent of Vesuvius, another 'must' as features unique of their kind in Europe), and from there they gravitated to Rome, Florence, and Venice (drinking punch at Florian's). . . . It took them ten days to return home via Parma, Verona, Turin, mail coach over the Mont Cenis, then steamer up the Sâone and train from Chalon to Paris.

Dickens was in managerial capacity and would not let Collins economise as much as he wanted. So the trip worked out at £126 1s 8d each, 10 October to 10 December; not as 'reasonable' as Wilkie and Egg had been led to expect. 'The expenses made the Neophytes wink a little,' was Dickens' comment. Sometimes they behaved in the aggravating English way, as in the wretched and dirty inn at Bolsena where 'we made a great fire and strengthened the country wine with some brandy (we always carry brandy) and mulled it with cloves (we always carry cloves) and went to bed, and got up before 5 and breakfasted on our own tea (we always carry tea) and came away in the dark'. (An earlier generation of travellers abroad had been advised to carry not only condiments, spices and tea, but knives, spoons and bed linen : Smollett took two and a half dozen spoons!) On the whole they simply travelled in a state of 'mad good spirits'.

On the Grand Tour manners, like company, had become more vulgar. Milor Anglais had been inclined to the grand, intent on the right introductions, a little aloof, but open-handed, French-speaking and prepared to accept the rough with the smooth. By mid-nineteenth century many middle-class travellers were about, speaking no language but their own, yet ever prepared to dispute their bills and accommodation, querulous about discomforts and ready to assume that all foreigners were either rogues or fools. 'Dicky' Doyle, *Punch* artist, poked gentle fun at the 'Great Briton' upon the Rhine or on the Grand Canal in the woodcuts of his *Foreign Tour of Brown, Jones and Robinson*, 1854. A cynic might say that they would have done better at home, leaving foreign parts to the dedicated 'sketchers and washers' like Lear or reading them up in one of the astonishingly full and vivid handbooks of conducted tours, such as *Walks in Rome*, regularly produced, at first for Murray and then other publishers, by Augustus Hare, who took a six weeks' continental tour, also in 1853, seeing the greater part of Germany and much of France, and even reaching Prague (still considered by some a 'half-barbaric, half-Asian city'), all for £25.

Yet already, as perhaps Lear's and Byron's departure have foreshadowed, while the Grand Tour was being diluted into popular tourism, another sort of tour was in the making. Its early communal exemplar was again 'plushy' : its company included three Christian ministers, eight doctors, sixteen or eighteen ladies, several military or naval chieftains, an ample crop of professors and a gentleman who had 'Commissioner of the United States of America to Europe, Asia and Africa' after his name. It was a novelty in the way of excursions, its like had not been thought of before, and in the prospectus issued from offices in Brooklyn it was advertised as 'Excursion to the Holy Land, Egypt, the Crimea, Greece and Intermediate Points of Interest', but 'the trip can be extended, and the route changed, by unanimous vote of the passengers'. It heralded a new wave of travellers, for whom Europe would no longer be the confines of the Grand Tour— though for *young* Americans Europe itself had only become a possibility with the steamships and railways. For it the 'very beautiful and substantial side-wheel steamship *Quaker City* had been chartered'. Travelling expenses ashore were calculated at five dollars a day in gold and the full passage cost $1,250.

This trip, which in one passenger's eyes had a justification more radical than that expressed by Dickens of the late Grand Tour : 'to see most of that extensive miscellany of objects, which it is essential that all persons of polite cultivation should see', was to acquire lasting fame in the guise of *The New Pilgrim's Progress* or *Innocents Abroad*. Mark Twain, the observant passenger, regarded it as an excursion desirable 'to be gotten up every year and the system regularly inaugurated. Travel is fatal to prejudice, bigotry and narrow-mindedness, and many of our people need it sorely on these accounts'.

With the *Quaker City* as their travelling base the pilgrims were
able to take Florence, Venice and Athens in their stride, 'do'
Constantinople, and then, having been warned to provide themselves with green spectacles and umbrellas, saddles (for Syrian
travel), veils (for Egypt) and substantial clothing (for roughing
it in the Holy Land) to swan out to Smyrna, Ephesus, Jerusalem
and Jericho before finally fetching up at Shepheard's Hotel, Cairo.
They were well-heeled and prepared to travel heavy, if not quite
in the Byronic tradition. They hired horses, dragomen, saloon
tents everywhere and considered comfort before expense. They
trailed in the wake of voluble and tireless guides and saw everything, from a letter by Christopher Colombus 'wis his own hand'
in the municipal palace at Genoa to the house of St Veronica in
Jerusalem, whose 'authentic' miraculous handkerchief the tourists
were shown in cathedrals in Paris, in Spain, in Milan and in
Rome at five francs a time. They made a sensation wherever
they went—none of them had ever been anywhere before—
standing on no ceremony or conventionality, but always taking
good care to make it understood that they were Americans. 'The
people stared at us everywhere and we stared at them.' They
were full of enthusiasm about the 'pilgrimage' part of the excursion, the Holy Land, 'we fairly rioted among the holy places
of Jerusalem'.

They came back with trophies and costumes of all sorts, from
everywhere they went, but as Twain reveals between the lines of
his hilarious account, the excursion was not quite the success
planned. He puts it down to the prevailing age-group of the
passengers, but could Augustus Hare's hint to travellers, in *Walks
in Rome* indicate another possible cause? 'There is one point
which cannot be sufficiently impressed on those who wish to take
away more than a mere surface impression; it is, never to see too
much; never try to "Do" Rome.' The innocents abroad did.

Three-quarters of the *Quaker City*'s passengers were between
forty and seventy years af age. Those from this side of the
Atlantic who followed in their wake, up to and after World War
I, were also likely to be nearer to the end than the beginning of
their earning careers. The pattern of this more expansive 'pro-

gress' abroad drew many 'Cookii', as Arabs called them.

But while the Holy Land attracted its new, sober-sided pilgrims and the Rhineland its young sparks on pleasure bent—
perhaps 'bummelling' with a bicycle in the fashion of 'George',
'Harris' and Jerome K. Jerome—horizons for the adventurous
further widened. The later nineteenth century saw the lady
traveller in the ascendant. Breaking their moral, legal and
domestic chains and breathing the heady air of the new freedom,
a few women pioneers now set their faces boldly towards the
East.

Isobel Arundel, of an aristocratic family, craving from girlhood
'gypsies, Bedouin and everything Eastern and mystic and especially a wild and lawless life', found what she desired in the Syrian
desert, in Jeddah, and in Portuguese India (Goa), as the wife of
Burton of Arabia. Jane Digby, who 'at seventy-four began to
find life in the tents too rough, the long desert rides too exhaust-
ing' started life at Holkham Hall, Norfolk in the Byronic age
and ended it at Damascus as wife of Sheikh Abdul Medjuel El
Megrab 'more Bedouin than the Bedawi'. She rode in tribal skirm-
ishes at the head of troops with her husband (the fourth), knew
Baghdad, Aleppo, Palmyra as well as the Paris of her youth, met
Lear on his way from Petra, and the Burtons, but not that other
desert Arabian, Doughty, and joyfully exchanged the western
way of life of 'have' or 'do' for the desert way of simply 'be'.
How different from the ladies with plaid shawls and 'waterproof
mackintosh life preservers' who had only recently come to rhap-
sodise over Bruges and Brussels, or even from 'Vernon Lee'
(Violet Paget) daringly touring Italy by bicycle, but being followed by a carriage with several pairs of boots and boot-trees!

There were other such emancipated lady travellers—and travellers manquées—like 'Laurence Hope', who wrote such poems
as 'Afridi Love' and 'The Night of Shiva', joined her husband
General Nicolson on north-west frontier reconnaissance and
shocked visiting memsahibs by her bare feet and unorthodox
dress. And especially, at the end of the century, there was Gertrude Bell, orientalist, naturalist and traveller of the first order.

As with her predecessors above, Gertrude Bell's initial advantage of family means and connections opened doors to her that would have stayed closed for many. Her grandfather was an ironmaster, colliery owner and FRS. She first went to Persia at the age of twenty-three when her uncle was Minister at Tehran. Thereafter the desert, 'miles and miles of it with *nothing* growing: ringed in with bare bleak mountains, snow-crowned and furrowed with the deep courses of torrents, a very wonderful thing to see', was her life's love. Exploration of its different aspects and fastnesses took her to Syria, the Hamad, Petra and Baalbeck, Mesopotamia, Carcemish, the Nejd, Hayil and many places besides, previously considered inaccessible to a European woman. At Carcemish, with its Hittite remains, she notes, May 1911 : 'I went there—it was only five hours ride—and found a young man called Lawrence (he is going to make a traveller).' T. E. Lawrence was wearing a red tasselled belt to his white flannel shorts, the sign of a bachelor in that region, and so it was decided by the Arab diggers that Gertrude was coming out to marry him. Subsequently her Syrian journeys were to provide Colonel Lawrence with much valuable information for the Arab campaigns of the last phase of the war.

Although in the pre-war decade, according to Murray's handbook for travellers in Asia Minor, Transcaucasia, Persia etc, a first class steamer passage from Manchester to Mersin, in southeast Anatolia, cost only £11, such journeys as the above were not for tourists, however adventurous—yet. Ladies were more likely to be observed, as by Arnold Bennett about 1910, 'nibbling daintily at crumbs of art and archaeology in special booklets which some of themselves have written and others of themselves have illustrated, and which make the coarse male turn with an almost animal satisfaction to Carl Baedeker', in Rome or Florence. Only exceptionally placed males like the Hon Aubrey Herbert (figured as Sandy Arbuthnot in John Buchan's Balkan-Turkish thriller *Greenmantle*) could meet a friend and decide 'in ten minutes conversation that we would try to reach Sanaa, the capital of the ancient Arabia Felix and of the modern province of Yemen'. He had already travelled in Albania, Greece, Turkey and Arabia, making friends everywhere 'with the most extraordinary heroes and ruffians'. Or like Lawrence himself (who first bicycled round France and then walked round in Syria looking at Crusader castles) could obtain introductions (to Doughty) and backing (from the archaeologist in charge at Carcemish) to give him a foothold in Syria for further wanderings south and east. They were the precursors.*

After World War I bright young men gave the European Grand Tour a stylish flip, before proceeding on their diverse ways in other fields. At twenty-five Beverley Nichols was already a seasoned traveller : his autobiography published at that age includes a journey to Greece, by train, via Fiume and Belgrade, 'the most sinister and the most melancholy of all the cities I have ever seen' (cities have tended to be 'the most' one thing or the other for young men abroad from Boswell on). But it is Athens which gets the treatment. Nichols describes the streets at night 'peopled with young giants in the most picturesque uniform of Europe' and 'dark swarthy people, with eyes like stars who do not so much walk as sway', among houses of white marble scattered with flowers and under a moon 'so clear and clean it might have been carved from the marble of the Acropolis'. And then the Acropolis itself, where 'among columns of dim silver, stained with shadows of violet, one is away from Time. The temples soar to the stars like white flowers eternally born anew', unless, as he characteristically inserts, 'I have inadvertently been describing a Lyceum pantomime'. This knock-down of one's own skittles of sentiment and rapture is something new.

Another young man, aged 21, Robert Byron—descended from a branch of the poet's family—made the Grand Tour itself as a jeu d'esprit in 1925, by Sunbeam touring car ('Diana') with two Oxford friends, from Grimsby via Germany and Italy to Athens. In *Europe through a Looking Glass* high spirits, high jinks and sense of comedy sometimes clash with his intent to offer a 'picture of the continent of which England forms a part' as a means of furthering the new sense of European consciousness; but certain

* Thomas Coryat, a parson's son from Somerset, must be considered an exception : in 1612 he toured the Middle East to India—taking in Smyrna, Aleppo, Jerusalem, Ecbatana (Hamadan), Isfahan, Lahore, Agra and ending up near Bombay.

things come clear. Byron and his friends, one from a banking and
ship-owning family, follow the old tradition, demanding always
'the best' of hotels and restaurants—no mixing here with 'the
English professional classes', treating regulations with amused
tolerance or defiance, seeing the contemporary Wandervögel as
a curious sub-species of travellers, and finding their welcome at
the Vatican Legation in Rome as warm as at the Petit Palais in
Athens. In short they revert to the ethos of the Age of Privilege,
but with one significant difference. Robert Byron had abnormally
acute powers of observation and a mind already stored with considerable knowledge of art and architecture, developed in forays
from Oxford. So he is alert to 'the culminating moment in the
Grand Tour of other days', the view that has so thrilled so many
artists and pilgrims to ecstasy—a first glimpse of Rome and the
dome of St Peter's rising, as it does from the plain, 'like some
huge mauve bulb out of the landscape'. But he is far more con-
cerned to pin down the exact colour of the buildings which help
to constitute Rome's charm—'a kind of dull burnt orange covered
with a roseate wash, yet at the same time the whole is flat and
restful. Towards sunset the tints become intensified to an extent
that one would have believed impossible outside the limelight of
Drury Lane'. At the Acropolis, where Nichols gushes, Byron
analyses. Having noticed, in passing, water-colour views of the
Parthenon depicted 'as a row of grooved cinnamon ninepins
against a sky the colour of a faded butcher's apron' and com-
mented on the sickening effect of Victorian sepia photographs
of Greek ruins, he brings the architectural splendour alive in
sharp objective phrases. The pillars are 'Doric, plain, massive
and fluted from top to bottom: the marble is as smooth as vellum,
its surface as hard as basalt, its edges as sharp as steel'; the sky
is brazen turquoise; the tall spike of Lycabettus rises from the
white blocks of the town beneath its veil of dust; in front the
chimneys and promontories of Piraeus; finally the sea and the
islands.

It is this 'attack' which makes Robert Byron the inspiring guide
for touring sophisticates later. When he transfers from Europe
and the Byzantine outpost, Mount Athos, to the Levant, Persia

and Afghanistan—now with a governing purpose : the quest for
the origins of Islamic art—his sharpened vision brings the romance of eastern travel down to bedrock reality. In the *Road to
Oxiana*, account of a journey from Venice to Balkh, he joins a
small company—Freya Stark, Rosita Forbes, and later Wilfrid
Blunt—who whet tourist appetites with that sense of hazards
lightly borne, unfamiliar cultures revealed and fresh sights found
worth the trouble of seeing, that is having its more general pay-
off only in this generation. Here Turkestan came vividly within
the reader's consciousness, if not his immediate range. Tabriz,
Shiraz, Meshed, Herat, Mazar-i-Sherif are the new names to
conjure with, no longer Ephesus, Aleppo, Petra, Jericho or even
Baghdad.

Robert Byron was fortunate, on his special quest, that the
mosques of Persia were just being furtively opened in the 1930s
and he was one of the first to report on the contents. His eye for
porcelain tile, mosaic, ivan, minaret, is as keen as for the archi-
tectonics of the Acropolis or the dynamics of Persepolis. He knows
the best and is not to be bamboozled. 'Mr Biron, one of the
learned-men of England is proceeding yours to pay visit to the
History buildings etc of that districts, who will also take photos of
the said buildings', reads one of his letters of introduction (from
Isfahan); and of course he finds old Etonian friends at legations
and has still a fine disregard for such people as travelling school-
masters. 'We were discussing the importance of comfort on our
journey. He [a schoolmaster] said he preferred discomfort,
revelled in it. I know the type, they die on one out of sheer in-
efficiency.' Byron does not, but he pioneers routes, as from Herat
into Turkestan, which involve both real hardship, hazard and
mental strain. His supports are whisky, Boswell, Thucydides and
a supply of detective stories. On these lengthy, remote, uncertain
journeys, 'journeys of supposed observation', the emphasis, he
thinks, should fall not so much on physical as on mental health.

I wish I were rich enough to endow a prize for the sensible
traveller, £10,000 for the first man to cover Marco Polo's out-
ward route reading three fresh books a week : and another

Page 35: (*above*) Xanthi, Macedonia; (*below*) at Canakkale, Dardanelles

Page 36 (*left*) Tombstone at the Museum of Ephesus, Selcuk; (*right*) graveyard at Eyup, Istanbul

£10,000 if he drinks a bottle of wine a day as well. That man
might tell one something about the journey. (*Road to Oxiana*)


'1949 May-June: Bahrain, Ridyadh, Kuwait, Basra, Bushira,
Shiraz, Isfahan, Chalus, Tabriz, Ruwunduz, Mosul, Urmia,
Baghdad.' The curriculum supplied by one of the post World
War II dedicated travellers, whose speciality was the Empty
Quarter of Arabia, is significant. To Wilfred Thesiger (*Arabian
Sands*) the world has shrunk: there are no more deserts, and
there can be no more explorers, only tourists. What was ten years
ago an almost unexplored area, such as Nuristan (Afghanistan),
complete with brigands, is now likely to have university expeditions waiting to go there or, in the desert, an encroaching
oil drill. But to the majority the former privileged world of the
dedicated traveller has opened out, really wide, for the first time.

As the opportunity of the old European Grand Tour filtered
down from the wealthy aristocrat to the middle class and even
the impecunious, if prepared for hardship, and as the circuit of
the Near East, popularised by Cooks and the other agencies, led
enterprising young Englishmen of the thirties to plan, as an
acquaintance of mine did, 'to walk to Jerusalem for Christmas',
so the chance to jump barriers of privilege or means and also of
remoteness, in the wake of such travellers as Robert Byron or
Rosita Forbes, came in the decade after World War II. To many
that war itself opened tantalising vistas of travel and glimpses of
alien cultures, and also familiarised them with living and moving
about in barren or outlandish places. Then bulldozers and jeeps
made or found roads where no roads for vehicles had been before. The possibilities were there: it needed only enterprise to
follow them up. The chance to outstrip in one venture all earlier
touring schemes, at minimal individual expense, came ten or
twelve years afterwards when the overland route through to India
was pioneered by young men with second-hand Land-Rovers and
first-hand experience of 'outback' conditions. The roads were
being further developed, with Russian or American aid, en route
to Afghanistan, dependable enough to repeat the venture with
passengers, by 'Dormobile' or sturdy second-hand coach. Light-

C

weight tents, self-cooking or communal messing kept down the expense. Two hundred years after *Sentimental Journey* the first wave of ordinary travellers could make the sensational journey, for *their* tour of a lifetime, not to Italy, but to and beyond the boundaries of India.

It seems fitting that after the former British and American waves of pilgrims it should now so often be the Australians who are involved in leading everyman to the older sites of civilisation. Not all 'personal column' offers of 'India Overland : young mixed party, three month round trip £150' or 'Kashmir and Nepal, small group expeditions leave May, June, Sept., October, ten weeks', set their sights on 'those objects which it is essential that all persons of polite cultivation should see', or even on being 'fatal to prejudice, bigotry and narrow-mindedness'. Their appeal is to adventuring or piling up visas in a passport. But in the chapters which follow it may be seen what opportunities exist, within the limits of such tours and their modern tempo, of making initial contact with other cultures and of beginning to put right a complaint which Aldous Huxley diagnosed in his eastern travel book *Jesting Pilate* :

> It is for its materialism that our western civilisation is generally blamed. Materialism, if it means a preoccupation with the actual world in which we live, is something wholly admirable. If western civilisation is unsatisfactory, that is not because we are interested in the actual world : it is because the majority of us are interested in such an absurdly small part of it.

# 2 THROUGH EUROPE

*The grand object of travelling is to see
the shores of the Mediterranean.*　　　Samuel Johnson

That mid-February day I wakened about six in the morning to
the sound of a tug-boat's hooter and a continuous noise like sails
flapping. It was still dark. I rolled over to get more sleep and
found I was lying on something hard, flat and gritty—in fact the
ground. What on earth? Then I remembered. The sail noise was
wind in tent flaps, the hooter came from a barge on the Seine
and I was on the first stage of a journey overland from England
to Nepal. We had pitched tents for a couple of nights in the Bois
de Boulogne on a site belonging to the Touring Club of France.

An hour or so later, we were all eating crusty chunks from
yard-long loaves or heating up soup on portable stoves, while the
rest of the camp came to life. For our party, camping wherever
possible, even in cities, meant money saved in Europe for the rest
of the journey into Asia, without having to miss the Baedeker
sights. We had ten or eleven weeks driving ahead of us and about
£1 each per day for expenses. Some of the bunch of young
Americans and Australians, New Zealanders and Canadians,
British and Irish who had found time to see the world, had
earned a 'Wanderjahr'; others had come to England to work for
a year or two and were now on their way home or else were
going to a job 'down under'. A few were going 'there and back'.
For everyone the 11,000 mile journey was the once-for-all trip
before settling down. For everyone except 'Sundowner' Bob, tall,
easy-going Australian driver and Frank, his relief, a wiry ex-
schoolmaster from New Zealand who acted as 'ginger-man' or

'bear-leader' to the party. To them it was another challenge of terrain, timing, tedium and tempers and a test for the MCW Leyland-engined coach.

Brussels, Paris, Lyons, Avignon, Marseilles, Nice, Monaco, Genoa, Mantua, Padua . . . Venice : our route is the well-worn and oft-described one. We enjoy it as an apéritif, shying now and again at the expense. Venice is our first major objective and the point at which those coming on from Germany or using Wagon-Lit service through France, if delayed in their start, can most easily join up.

Fortunately it is still off season, before swarms of tourists come to tarnish the 'universal dream'. For those who have seen it before only in pictures by Guardi or Canaletto, views of the Piazza San Marco or of the Piazzetta and its two monolith columns, the reality seems scarcely changed. The colours, the buildings in grey, pink or ox-blood, the umbrella'd stalls, the groups of strollers, the light from sea and sky, all charm with a sense of recognition. Façades of Renaissance elegance, fantasies of Gothic and By-zantine architecture, click into their expected places. Here, one says, time has stood still. Even the red cap or sailor's blouse, the red gown or stocking that Canaletto introduced among his blue, browns and grey-greens, is 'on stage'. A group forms before the superb painted archway into the Basilica—three of the Guardia Nationale in peaked black hats and long black cloaks, a child in a red cloak and hood with her mother also in a red coat, zebra stripes of sunlight and shadow fall across the flagstones, there are clouds of glossy pigeons. It is a magnificent set with San Giorgio 'rising like a fairy palace out of the sea' as backcloth.

People move across the piazza like stage crowds. An old man with a set of large, brightly coloured balls; a flock of clerks in black suits and hats hurrying to work; a child in charming *festa* costume—blue silk crinoline, blue shoes, white silk stockings, white stole, silvery-white wig and round posy of flowers; three tonsured monks in brown habits and black beards; a tall Ameri-can in bold-check trouser suit, draped sable coat, white glacé boots and floppy-brimmed felt hat who stands and poses as for an audience.

St Mark's Square is the city's drawing-room, open for anyone to sit and stare, sure to contain his friends in the course of a day either feeding the pigeons, waiting for the hour of the automata to strike on the blue clock, or listening to the café orchestras playing old Viennese waltzes—just as at one time everybody who was anybody in Europe was sure to be seen some day or other at Florian's.

Of the two ways of seeing Venice: limiting exploration to the Grand Canal, St Mark's and the Lido, or searching out in the labyrinth of lanes and side canals its innumerable treasures of art and architecture, we kept (on Hare's principle) to the first. The second way spells despair if one wants briefly to achieve any sort of impression of the whole.

From St Mark's we take the sweep of the Grand Canal on foot, having already had our first sight of the palaces and their lovely broken liquid reflections from the 'vaporetto'. We loiter through the serpentine Merceria, one of Venice's few landways justifying the title of street, and admire its stylish, expensive shops. We exchange looks with the knowingly smiling statue in Campo San Bartolomeo. We savour the Latin flavour of the cinema stills, TUTTO PER AMORE, and the high gloss and operatic, oval-framed artistry of the posters. We cross the Ponte di Rialto and are held fascinated by the squids, folpi, scampi, eels, trout, sild, sepia, oysters, mussels, razor-shell fish, shrimps, live crayfish and tunny in the market. We dodge balloon-sellers, peanut-sellers, sellers of postcards, of Venetian glass, the first trickle of German tourists, nuns in white, monks in brown, priests in shovel hats, porters with leaning head-piles of baskets, gondoliers with gold teeth touting for custom—and by devious turns reach the Strada Nuova from which the way lies reasonably clear to Lista di Spagna and the Scalzi bridge.

We are riveted by the displays of pizza, tosti, strudel, in the confectioners' and the voluptuous pyramids of pears, apples, lemons, mandarins, tangerines, artichokes, asparagus, aubergines on the open stalls. We buy bunches of English-spring-smelling primroses from a countrywoman with basket and shawl and linger among the book barrows of San Leonardo, tempted by the

gay paper-covered duodecimos of ROMEO E GIULIETTA with a
Venetian imprint. After a beer among the porters and boatmen
near the Canale di Cannaregio we wander into narrow alleyways
of high tenements, with their curly iron balconies, precarious
flower-pots, carved stone heads and plaques, where washing
flutters like streamers between upper floors and green water rip-
ples along old walls and under humped stone bridges. Craftsmen's
workshops and sunny squares lie in wait round every corner.

With Casanova's Palace, the Querini Palace and Tintoretto's
'Assembly of the Blest' (largest picture ever painted on canvas);
with the magnificent gilded roof mosaics in the umber dusk of
San Marco (Ruskin's 'golden caverns of St Mark's') and its four
great antique bronze horses (stolen from Constantinople) prancing above the entrance; with the most famous small bridge in the
world, the Bridge of Sighs, and the glittering waterfront, we are
almost sated by excess of sensuous enjoyment when Byron's
Lido beckons. So another day for following the poet, if not his
example, in 'rowing to the Lido with two singers, one of whom
was a carpenter and the other a gondolier: the recitative was
shrill, screaming and monotonous, and the gondolier behind
assisted his voice by holding his hand to one side of his mouth,
while the carpenter prompted him with the verses of Tasso's
Jerusalem.' Instead we join company in the Trattoria Roma and
exchange one sensuous enjoyment for another—minestrone,
trout, salad, bel paese, a perfectly ripened pear and a flask of
soave bianco. . . .

Two days in Venice: comparable to spending five minutes in
the National Gallery. There is time for a long second look at the
most romantic waterfront in the world—the Doge's palace, dazzling triumph of Gothic or Saracenic architecture, the green-
gleaming dome and Palladian front of San Giorgio Maggiore, the
black-velvet cut shapes of gondolas against the sun, the clusters
of striped mooring-posts, great barbers' poles with glittering
points. We lean over the warm marble balustrade of the Rialto
bridge carved with the hearts and initials of innumerable Romeos,
to imagine the gilt and scarlet splendour of a regatta, all banners
and painted prows and gondoliers in full pomp. We enjoy an-

other toasted pizza, buy trifles of red Venetian glass, drink another bitter Campari and watch the steamers, with the green lion of St Mark's on their funnels, disgorge parties of nuns and school-girls, while the dapper officers strut along the waterfront. We smell the 'unforgettable, unforgotten' odour of the canals (sewage filtered through sea water), glimpse the piani nobili of old palaces and try to fix in memory the half-oriental half white-iced wed-ding-cake effect of St Mark's. We brood yet again over the Bridge of Sighs' reflections of wet crumbling stone in constantly mov-ing water, marvel at the overwhelming public splendour and opulence of the Venetian past. Our last look is taken from the Campanile where the whole network of canals, the lagoon, the Lido and in the distance the Adriatic, swim into view, a view even more glorious than those familiar masterpieces by Guardi and Canaletto.

No one wants to leave Venice—save our drivers. But next day we whistle along the Golfo di Venezia, with calm blue sea, pale blue sky, towering limestone crags and cut-through road tunnels, and over the Venetian plain of cornlands and rich orchards; then along the Golfo di Trieste, past Miramare—a kind of Adriatic Balmoral—and arrive in Trieste that un-Italian city, before the image of Venice has had time to fade.

Trieste is a cold douche of reality. Trams, tall bleak office blocks, granite banks and public buildings, a funicular railway, dockyards, endless houses piled up between sea and bare sur-rounding hills. In the square there are four great stone building masses with arched entries resembling the gladiatorial tunnels into the arena; a vast road works excavation is in progress and there is a suspicion of drizzle. Altogether an uncompromising Hapsburgian place, exile for James Joyce, semi-exile for Consul Richard Burton. Only the umbrella'd market stalls and the fish-ing boats by the land-locked quay have Italian warmth and colour.

Shortly Frank comes through the coach collecting passports, the Australian, American, New Zealand, Canadian, Irish and British in separate piles to speed frontier procedure. . . . Customs already: the carnet for the coach, change of currency, spending up 'little money' on cigarettes or sweets. We loiter between the barriers, idly watching officials search the cars, and noting their occupants' reactions. Those who act up, try the high horse, get the full treatment—all cases turned out, door pockets, glove compartments, upholstery thoroughly searched. We are luckier, not 'stretched upon the rack at the customs house' as the traveller complained in Napoleon's day. Half an hour sees us on our way.

Yugoslavia offers what our Canadians call 'big country'. Oak and fir woods, deer-run hills, still powdered with snow, deep winding gorges, long rolling plough land and maize fields, withdrawn villages and tall narrow church towers with slender pierced spires and, above all, the great central massif of ice-capped mountain, suggest the homeland of a tough race. Down avenues of white poplars we pass cumbrous ox-carts and horse-drawn waggons; cattle are being driven into the yards of solid, buff-brown farms with open colonnades and barns of rough-hewn stone. Most houses have steep, broad eaves like Swiss chalets. The church towers vary in colour from village to village; from lemon, cream, peach to silver-grey and black : their spires and cupolas, guiding fingers to villages in the combes of the hills, show every inventive fancy of design.

Ljubljana, first stop in the SOCIALISTIKA FEDERATIVA, surprises everyone. Its importance as a cross-roads dates from its Roman days as 'Emona' : its situation on the river Ljubljanica with red stone medieval castle towering above it gives it a Salzburgian air. But the old quarter of narrow streets overhung by gables, of cobbled squares, baroque buildings and frescoed churches is less of a museum piece than old Salzburg.

We stroll past the antique shops, full of carved wooden dolls, ikons and blunderbusses, cross the river by a beautiful stone bridge and admire the Bruges-like waterside and reflections; then wander past the herb market, set up under an open colonnade, where every kind of culinary spice and 'cure' is displayed in neat wooden bowls or jars. We look into the butter, cheese and bacon market, situated half underground between cool stone arches; we skirt the open fruit and flower stalls, where the Slovene dress is as bright as the striped awnings. We savour the juxtaposition of Teutonic gables, copper-green domes, gilded frescoes, stone colonnades and the special 'feel' of a town where theatre, opera house, art gallery, museum are integral and alive. We return to take another look at the bridge, golden drooping willows and long colonnade. . . .

Down the long swinging loops of the autoput, through a land-scape of vast fields, fir plantations and wide, white-sanded river beds we move now at speed. Occasionally the pale green, pink or white tower of a church and the red or bright green terra-cotta tiles of its spire flash their signal of nearby habitation. Once a bundle of box-wood tied to a post indicates a roadside inn : 'good wine needs no bush'. There is a distant view of blue hills beyond the Sava river, whose course we are following. The slivovic circulates. Some of us begin to acquire that remote afternoon gaze.

The road stretches on and on. It is dusk when we draw up in Zagreb, some 250 miles from Venice. A half moon is up and hoar frost sparkles in the grass. A motel is indicated for the night.

We enjoy the comforts of People's Tourism—fierce steam heating, spartan chambres à deux, scalding showers and a view from the windows of blocks of workers' flats, grey oblong factories, concrete truck parking lots and greyish scrub, quite apart from the old Austrian town; Picasso reproductions and pot plants on the landing, crackling TV in the cafeteria. Food and wine are cheap : the waitresses in white rubber ankle boots, pretty but serious or a trifle unsympathetic to our non-party line. Soup, pork chops, fried potatoes, cabbage and beetroot salad, apple strudel and a tot of slivovic cost about five shillings. In the bed-room we turn off sizzling radiators and try to open a window. It gives only a couple of inches, but the icy draught is enough—straight from the Steppes. We close it and suffocate.

From Zagreb to Belgrade the autoput cuts straight through like an arrow on a campaign map—'line for exploitation through the Ljubljana Gap into the plains of Hungary'—in this case ex-ploiting the flood plain of the Sava. Iced-over marsh, red reeds, sedges with heads like washing-up mops, sparse herds of sheep and goats, frequent over-turned trucks (had their drivers dozed off from the monotony?), poplars lining the river and earth side-roads, multitudes of magpies, rooks and hooded crows—these are the components of the scene. The villages are too far away to appreciate, but their inhabitants appear at intervals; whole families labouring on the narrow strips of unfenced fields, men behind the plough, women leading the plough-oxen or pushing loaded barrows, grannies in charge of flocks while spinning wool from distaffs. Heavy loads are carried on poles, fore and aft over a shoulder, or by donkeys, down the trodden earth tracks. Carts have high wooden sides like haywains. Food has been brought to eat beside the dykes or in the lee of a maize stack, not unpleasant in spring, but spring's only signs so far are a few sparse drifts of primroses on sheltered banks and an occasional hedge of yellow forsythia.

We reach Belgrade by mid-afternoon, a sprawling city of three quarters of a million people. At best it apes Paris, with a layout of tree-lined avenues, tall grey public buildings, statuary, gardens and café squares. But not in its sombre air, serious crowds in subfusc clothes, its lack of wheeled traffic and its trailing off into small dimly-lit one-room shops and shanties. A wind like a hack-saw now harries the pedestrians with dust and grit as they hurry by, close to the walls.

We walk out to the castle. The grey, dried-out grass in the grounds looks as though it would never be green again. The grey bulk of a work by the famous Yugoslav sculptor Ivan Mestrovic dominates the approach; in the dry moat beyond are ranged huge grey museum pieces of artillery. From the walls we look out on the confluence of the Danube and the Sava : both are grey, a darker grey than the tall concrete blocks of flats of Novi Beo-grad, the new town biting into the endless Pannonian plain. In high summer, no doubt, with its fountains playing, roses out, strolling couples on the ramparts, cafés busy and the Danube's blue restored, Belgrade cheers up, becomes less flavourless.

Across the river a large new building, with sharp-angled three-storeyed bays like the hulls of a glass fleet at mooring, flashed brightly. We fought a way over the bridge against the wind and entered a warm haven for the rest of the day. The collection of impressionists, dadaists and surrealists, the displays of folk art and abstracts, the wealth of sculpture in wood, stone and metal were admirably displayed and would alone put Belgrade today on the cultural map.

Another cold morning. We soar along by the river Juzna Morava, between wintry fields, skim ice pools and snow-veined hills, with a lacquer frieze of peasants, two-wheel carts, donkeys, herds of pigs and sheep being driven to market. Villages, fenced with wattle, knotting together their pantiled cottages along narrow muddy lanes, are the only habitations until Nis. Here market is in full swing. Brown-faced women in white coifs, bodices with flower embroidery or gay designs of coloured material, deep purple skirts or baggy Turkish trousers and cross-laced sheepskin shoes, stand behind their mounds of apples, red peppers, garlic, leeks and onions. Men in flat caps and leather-padded waistcoats lead pigs tied by one leg. A veteran comes up to us of fine aquiline features, russet skin, sweeping white moustaches, tall fur cap and sheepskin waistcoat worn fleece inwards. He is anxious to talk, but as dumb in any language that we know as we in his. He conducts us to the old fortress, where a mosque, Turkish baths and an ossuary of the Serbo-Croat war are now enclosed in public gardens. The town's turbulent history, going back to the time when it was the summer residence of Constantine the Great, has left it many such monuments. Most remarkable is the Skull Tower, in whose walls the Turks placed the heads of Serbian warriors fallen in the first insurrection against Turkish dominion. Freedom was achieved only in 1912 when Macedonia was divided between Serbs, Bulgars and Greeks.

Towards Skopje the countryside is more picturesque; shapely hills, brawling rivers between yellow-green willows, red-roofed villages on the slopes or by the water with tracks winding out to them over bare brown soil, in the distance the snow-covered Julian Alps. Skopje itself is Macedonia's economic and cultural centre, city of open air cafés chantants, Tzigane bands, green lawns and river promenades, with a fifteenth-century mosque and bridge and a sixth-century fortress floodlit at dusk. It is still obviously rebuilding after the devastating earthquake of 1963.

The surviving part of the old quarter has its own decrepit fascination. Narrow streets of jewel-repairers, silversmiths, brass vendors, sandal-makers, photographers, cap shops—in fur, felt, cloth, tweed check and beret style—bookstalls, lemonade, yoghourt and sweetmeat stalls, all hugger-mugger below the leaning tower of an old church, lead to the earthen square of the market-place. Women in blue trousers bend double under baskets of washing, Arabs in grey skullcaps hump sacks full of old papers and carpet, street lamps carry black-bordered notices of recent deaths and condolences received. Brightest spot is a cobbler's shop, with a gossiping group inside and the walls plastered with film posters, postcards and photos of Taylor, Bardot, Loren, Lollobrigida.

Across the square swarms a Sunday-at-Hyde-Park-corner crowd, with the difference that this is wholly Slav, male and all in drab-coloured suits. It fills the wide thoroughfare with a solid milling mass. This is the Saturday night outing for men, who walk endlessly up and down between ruined railway station and river, greeting their friends. We watch them over our self-service meal of mutton stew and jam pancakes at a People's Restaurant.

Flowering wild cherries clotted like snowflakes on the road-sides or clustered in drifts among the sulphur-yellow trunks of the sprayed orchards as we followed the course of the river Vardar. The river plain lacks feature as far as Titov Veles, a silk and porcelain centre, but the town itself has an attractive situation, straddling the river Vardar, slate-green now between rugged hills, with a ganglion of mosque, russet roofs, cream-plastered walls and mud-brick houses extending up the slopes. The streets were thronged again with men and boys in dark Sunday best suits, waiting for the cinemas to open. We admired, by contrast, the boy dressed in bright blue, sitting on a white mule behind a load of yellow straw covered with a pink cloth.

Beyond the town the Vardar pushes its way through two long, winding gorges where fishermen were standing in the sandy shoals of the flood overflow, up to their thighs. At Stobi, an old Greek town, the confluence of the Vardar with the Reka gives the river a majestic width. In the upper reaches it flows through rich summer fields of tobacco, cotton and poppy; in the lower reaches it is surrounded by the largest vineyards of Yugoslavia—the reason why our bottles of 'negro' or 'belo' were so inexpensive in Skopje. After Gradsko and a third magnificent rocky gorge the river enters the great fertile plain that extends to Gevgelya and the Greek border.

As soon as we cross the border—or even just before—all feel the change. The light takes on a special clarity, the landscape a clean symmetry, the buildings those bright primary colours and the sentries a particular panache only found in Greece. 'The vibrating air of the mountains, the heat and light of the plains, the dazzle of the sun on the sea' are to come. But instead of the drab, clumsy-gaited soldiery seen in every Yugoslav town, here in a raised red, blue and white sentry box is an upstanding Cozone, tall, strong-legged, bronzed, in striking uniform of stout shoes with pompoms, white tights, short kilt, dark blue Zouave jacket, and red tasselled cap, holding rifle and bayonet tautly at the slope under the fluttering blue-and-white flag.

At Polycastron, the first village, every feature seems right. A farm with whiter-than-white porch and bright blue walls, a white-haired lady in black at the door spinning, a golden-brown cock, a speckled hen and a white cat in the sun under a trellised vine; men sitting on rush-bottomed chairs outside a cafeneion—the coffeeshop, club and newsroom of every Greek village—taking their ouzo or tiny cups of Turkish coffee. Shops are painted white, light blue or sea-green : in the sandy square a bearded priest in black robe and gas-stove hat, his hair done up behind in a bun, walks sedately with two young girls. And over all a fresh brilliance of light.

Thessaloniki, second city of Greece, two thousand years old, second capital of the Byzantine Empire, with half a million people, offers several surprises. Among them are its monuments, its fourth-century acropolis, its mosaics and what look like its fourth-century roads.

The roads first. Apart from the main traffic-snarled thoroughfare and its avenues branching off to the sea front, they are at best of uneven hard-packed earth, with tilting pavements of broken concrete : at worst they might be stony gullies left by a torrent, full of rubble, deep ruts and half-buried boulders. Some have discontinued excavations for archaeological remains; for others mere antiquity seems to be the sole excuse. After dark, as pitfalls for unwary consumers of ouzo or mavrodaphne, they are one hundred per cent effective.

I walked up through some of these roads and streets, not far from Aristotle University, to reach a high viewpoint. Saddlers and carpet-sellers, tinsmiths and coppersmiths, chain- and tool-makers lined the way, varied with nut and cachou vendors, fruit and vegetable stalls, shops selling the famous 'baklavas' or halvas (a Turkish delicacy) and stray curio shops stacked with garish amphoras of pseudo-Attic design. Beyond the last cobbler's, now with portraits of Colonel Grivas and General Metaxas alongside Gina or Brigitte, I found a cobbled street which bent a hairpin course steadily uphill. A local bus crunched round the blind corners, missing donkey-drawn milk carts and motor-cycle trade vans by a coat of paint. The houses on each side were coloured like children's bricks—pink, green, yellow, red, orange, dark or light blue, dazzling white, their terra-cotta pantiles held down by large stones. Nearly all had a minute garden, pump or white-washed wall, half a dozen birdcages hoisted up by pulleys, pot plants on the steps, a flowering cherry tree or two and a chair out in a sunny corner. Some of the larger old wooden houses had an oriental aspect. Their solaria, traditional from medieval times, their use of indented projections to give spaces correct orienta-tion, their heavy ornate shutters, walled courtyards behind tall green double doors, with brass knockers in the form of a half-closed hand (a pattern popular in Isfahan also)—these belonged to the times when a man's habitation constituted his refuge and his family's closed universe, and recalled Thessaloniki's five cen-turies of Turkish occupation. Here was a village within a city.

At an upper level the winding street burgeoned with bake-houses, wash-houses, small tailors and repairers, then, rounding a last corner, it dived through the gateway of the old walls. This is the approach to Eptapyrgion, the acropolis, whose fourth-

century ramparts and crumbling redoubts give shelter to shepherds' flocks and gypsy squatters, After enjoying things in the
Greek way—white bread, white butter, a white cheese, olives and
retsina in a copper can, in the vine-shaded courtyard of the inn,
with the acropolis in view, I was fortified for the climb to Eptapyrgion's highest point. A vast city, basilicas, rotundas, mosques,
a solitary minaret, a great sixteenth-century sea tower, thronged
streets, impressive port and harbour works spread gleaming below. Away to the south across the wine-dark Aegean rose the
magnificent head of Mount Olympus, Zeus' throne, snowy white
and capped by puffs of cloud. To climb, as usual, proved its
worth.

Thessaloniki has thirty-five notable churches, Byzantine, post-
Byzantine and Moslem, and within them remarkable frescoes
and Christian mosaics. On returning from the upper to the
modern city I took in one, the massive, crudely simple Rotunda
of St George. Probably erected by the Emperor Galerius, who
triumphed over the Persians in AD 297, it was converted into a
Christian church about a hundred years later; the great brick-
built dome and the lateral arches glow with mosaics and gold.
The whole roof interior seems to flower, green, blue, red, purple
with a rich, recondite life of its own. As St George's is a store
museum the recesses are also crowded with interest: Graeco-
Roman statuary, pottery, plaques of various periods, and the
surrounding graveyard contains tombs of all styles and inscriptions. An archbishop's tomb with carved crozier, mitre and inscription in classical Greek; a Roman family tombstone with a
figure resting on a triclinium, a table set and handmaid serving;
box-tombs and headstones with carved sprays of flowers; mythical
figures, half man, half animal; a lovely naked boy, twin cherubs,
a Roman capital and columns of various marbles, some twisted
like barley sugar; delicate Arabic designs and inscriptions. One
could have loitered there half a day amidst the warm old stone
and at the arch of Galerius nearby, a massive pinky-cream monument to his legions' triumph, with near life-size bas-reliefs.

I steered for the sea front, down a boulevard dotted with glass
booths selling newspapers, sweets, tobacco, toothpaste, combs,

romantic novelettes with Byronic heroes in red and yellow, pin-up magazines called ΣΤΡΙΠΤΗΣΕ or ΓΥΝΑΙΚΑ, and offering facilities for telephoning. There were grill-rooms where the chef turned the meat on a spit like a big bobbin over charcoal by the door and the menus included stuffed vine leaves and 'ladies'-fingers.' On the front all the cafés were full of black-suited men playing dominoes, backgammon, chess, cards or cribbage, over a coffee or glass of water and sugar cake. Some sat outside in over-coats and scarves, magnetised by that view across the Aegean to Olympus and by the movement of boats. The lights in the cinemas were coming on to reveal 'Hornblower', 'Ulysses', 'Bond Story', 'Tarzan', 'Mau-Mau', and a sprinkling of Greek Resist-ance heroics. Aesthetically this east-west axis of the city seemed banal : so far as buildings go Thessaloniki's past clearly dwarfs its foreseeable future.

The road out as far as Pella, birthplace of Alexander the Great and former capital of Macedonia, meant a short return on our tracks. We crossed the river Axios, our old friend the Vardar, which has carried down so much silt that over the years Pella, an original coastal town, now stands fifteen miles from the sea. From there we turned south to Athens.

In Greece they say it is spring time all the year round. As we swung down to Katerini across the clean, ringing plain, black-dressed women rode donkeys side-saddle to market and in every village square 'parliament' was in session : black-clad men on café chairs under gnarled, heavily pruned trees discussing news and views and ouzo. The air became more and more crystalline : the sea took on a hyacinthine shade of blue. Greece opened up, 'chiselled out of its own light'. And now, just over a road crest, soared Mount Olympus, home of the Gods, with a summit of brilliant snowy splendour lifting above the fleecy cloud layer to 9,570 feet.

Cape Platamon, of camping renown for its beach and over-hanging fortress, and the river Peneus, lay beyond. Then we were entering the defile of the Vale of Tempe, between Olympus and Mount Ossa, where Aphrodite, Artemis and Daphne bathed in the legendary springs and we were soon romping down to Lárisa.

Page 53: (left) at Pierre
Loti Kahvesi, Eyup;
(right) Fisherman at Gal-
lipoli

Page 54 : (*above*) Eceabat, Dardanelles; (*below*) Soltani Madraseh, Isfahan

Much of this route is up to motorway standard—with a toll—and so far involved little or no climbing.

After Lárisa, we crossed a magnificent rolling plain bounded by distant ranges, a countryside of Homeric proportion, and dotted with great herds of horses, as far as Farsala. It was the kind of country where 'geography and nature itself assume forms that are perfectly proportioned to the stature and energies of man'. Then in a sudden series of sharp, tight backloops, we were climbing the flank of Mount Othrys to the pass at 1,600ft. From it we looked back across a wide and splendid olive-green landscape. This, of course, was Thessaly, celebrated in classical times for its cavalry, with great fields of pasture and some arable stretching as far as sight could follow. Farsala, or Pharsalos, is the ground where Julius Caesar won his victory over Pompey the Great.

On the crags at the side of the pass ΖΗΤΟ Ο ΣΤΡΑΤΟΣ, ΖΗΤΟ ΒΑΣΙΛΕΥΣ had been whitewashed or laid out in white stones—'Long live the Army', 'Long live the King', and, more poignantly, ΕΛΛΑΣ ΠΡΟΜΑΧΟΣ 'Greece the Champion' (of Freedom), reminder of guerrilla fighting. But the curly-haired shepherd by the roadside, with his leaping black and brown goats, was a figure, like Thomas Hardy's ploughman, going back beyond the reach of wars. Lamia called a halt. We basked in the bright sun in one of the squares, with a coffee and loukoumi (Turkish delight), watching life go by—purple-and black-garbed priests, pigtailed schoolgirls, women street-sweepers, shoppers and sleek businessmen fiddling with their beads. We bought lunch rations, cream cheese and plump black olives, bread and retsina, dates, apples, oranges and treacle pastries. We noted, for 'next time', the hotel ΥΠΝΟΥ with a sunny balcony over the quieter end of the square. What could be more persuasive of traveller's rest than a hotel 'of sleep'?

After leaving Lamia the road ran straight as an arrow between shady bordering trees across the Spercheus river plain, turning roughish after Brallos. Then it became Alpine—though not with an Alpine road surface. In extraordinary loops and hairpins, baffling all sense of direction as it crossed side gorges, it climbed

D

severely through boulders, pot-holes, earth-slides and clinging red
mud, sometimes with a loose sandy surface, sometimes with a
stretch of new tarmac, to skirt the west flank of Mount Parnassus.
This was the road that the Spartans had used to reach their
stronghold against the Persian invader, at the north end of the
Pass of Thermopylae.

There was a dramatic defile to pass through, deep glens and
corries falling away to right and left, heart-lifting views of the
Vardoussia mountains and a biting air from snowy peaks of
about 8,oooft. Shepherds on foot could make quicker progress
than even a car, knowing how to scramble up and down hill,
cutting off the huge bends and corners. The MCW was a chancy,
unwieldy vehicle to swing about, dodging new rock-falls, pot-
holes and crumbling verges. The descent to Amphissa was as
exciting as the climb and varied with dense fir woods, villages
perched along the valley contours opposite, all yellow and red
pantiles and the occasional white church with gleaming campanile. At the farms ponies or pack mules stood tethered under
vine shade, black pigs rooted and jostled, a goatherd tended his
flocks, some with straight horns a foot long, others wearing bells.
There were blue bee-hives and a blue and white wayside shrine.
Far down below, the river bed looked nearly dried up already,
with only a little cloudy water running through.

From Amphissa we drove under the shade of olive trees straight
to Khrysson, another pantiled, golden village, with mossy roadside well and women carrying pitchers of water on their heads
up steep cobbled lanes. Cypress trees framed its brilliant white
Byzantine church with bright blue dome. Then came the final
tortuous climb, now on well-surfaced road, to Delphi. All else
apart Delphi has probably the most splendid camp-site in Europe.
We were late and took the hostel.

The best time for seeing Delphi is the cool quiet of early
morning. Most expectation-arousing, *and* satisfying, of places, a
legend, a shrine, the 'navel of the earth', the nadir of scenic
grandeur and mystery, it is still an attractive tidy village (population 6oo) despite its increasing spread of hotels.

We wake to the musical tinkling of bells and the gentle sound

of hooves, as donkeys and mules are led down the street at day-
break to work on the valley slopes. Across the plateau the cliffs
of Parnassus, the Phaedriades or Shining Rocks—of which one
turns rose in the dawn light, one fiery red in the late afternoon—
tower almost vertically into the sky, split by the cleft from which
issues the Castalián Spring. The way to the sanctuary retains the
old landmarks—the gate of the walls, the rough stones of the
Sacred Way, the site of the treasuries, the Sibylline rocks—all
excavated from under the Byzantine village that was built over it.
Only the magnificent statues and monuments are missing, carried
off in hundreds during the time of the Emperor Nero.

The Temple of Apollo, shrine and oracle, stands on a vast
natural stage against this background of cliffs. Its columns glint
with the stone's unquenchable lights of gold, ochre and rose.
Above the temple are the stadium and theatre, hewn directly
from the rock, where the sacred dramas and games commemorat-
ing Apollo's victory over the Python, first guardian of the oracle,
took place. Below the plateau and the narrow ribbon of road,
olive slopes drop away dramatically into Pleistos gorge, dark with
firs. At its lip, dappled in blue-green and olive-grey shadow, the
circular Tholos arrests the light, three slender white columns of
the rotunda's original twenty, surmounted by delicate carved
reliefs on the frieze. All is airy space, pure light, mysterious shade
and morning silence. A great, gnarled, ageless olive leans its bulk
across the stony path. One almost expects some nymph, pursued
by Pan, to round the corner. When had the oracle spoken last—
sixteen hundred years ago? It might have been yesterday.

From Delphi village we walked down to Khrysson, facing the
sun and a bay of the Gulf of Corinth. The rough track below the
hostel snaked among rock and red earth, prickly pear and close
tangles of spiny shrub. Pale blue scillas, dark blue grape hya-
cinths, tiny dark iris, pink, blue and mauve anemones, white
stars of garlic, single marigolds, grass of Parnassus and greeny-
yellow euphorbia clustered on every patch of turf or shade.
Among the rocks there were saxifrages, Alpine speedwell and
monk's cowl lilies. A sequestered church was flanked by blossom-
ing pink almonds; its graveyard was full of dazzling white crosses

and headstones, each with a niche for the jar of oil, water, incense
and family photograph. Tin lanterns hung over the graves and
wreaths of bright plastic flowers. I looked for the obol too, the
coin offered in classical times to Charon for ferrying the souls of
the dead across the Styx. There *was* a small coin—probably for
the next fill of oil.

We emerged at last on to a grassy plateau where donkeys
grazed and cats basked on crumbling walls. A sunny lane, shaded
by crabbed trees, led down by angles to the well-head in the tiny
square. The same women in black carried their water-pots. The
men, as always, sat outside the tavern on rush-bottomed chairs.
A priest in his black robe and dark blue soutane hob-nobbed from
group to group. A skein of shy schoolgirls in blue smocks and
harlequin stockings ran across. The tavern received us with surprise but open arms. ΚΑΛ' ΗΜΕΡΑ,   Khrysson!

All leave Delphi reluctantly—through the village street, past
the Shining Rocks and Apollo's Temple, skirting the gorge of
Pleistos and into the narrow ways of Arachova, where rugs and
carpets, skins and furs hang from every shop and wall-top like
gaily coloured flags. Their makers and sellers smile and beckon
us to stop. Surprisingly so high up there are vineyards: the
resinated red wine we had drunk at Khrysson is made in Arachova. Before these heights are left behind we come to the lonely
cross-roads where Oedipus unknowingly met and slew his father
Laius. Then in no time we are among the corn and cotton levels
of Levadhia and enter the great plain of Boeotia that sweeps
down under the slopes of Mount Helicon to the sea.

Thebes, now a sleepy country town, once the royal home of
Oedipus and his wife/mother and scene of the disclosure of his
double crime, leads us in to the national highway. It is flat and
fast, and less than four hours after leaving Delphi we are entering
the dusty, brown-hazed suburbs, the vista 'diced like an agglomeration of square white bricks' of modern Athens.

Hostel, cheap hotel in the Plaka or mod cons in Menander
Street, near neighbour of Euripides, Sophocles and Socrates
streets, provide choice of accommodation. Those choosing mod
cons are also close to Plateia Omonoia (where the Underground

begins), with its gamy flavour of Soho and elusive sound of bou-
zouki music from cellar cafés.

The Plaka, oldest part of Athens, is a more countrified Mont-
martre. It has white lanes of cobbled steps, taverns whose thick
vine branches writhe across the street like dark pythons, secretive
old houses, window shutters painted blue or red or green, pots of
basil in windows, smells of resin and charcoal and breathtaking
views of Lykabettos. Near at hand is the 'Flea Market', selling
everything from GI helmets, Singer sewing machines, old steam
irons, basket chairs, buckets made out of old tyres, to Russian
ikons, Nankin ware, bronze Buddhas, rare books and pop records.
The workshops of brass, tin and white-metal smiths surround it :
there are skivers' shops and a whole row of shoe- and sandal-
makers. One of them stacks a window with his own books, and
calls himself the foster-brother of Omar Khayyám.

Beyond all this lies the night-club quarter, decorated with
streamers and bunting, huge grotesque masks and papiermâché
figures, and with the ubiquitous display of antiquités. The mixture of smart décor, gimcrack novelty and dusty decay, with
glimpses between of ancient grandeur, has a savour all its own.

Among the white-washed cottages, fig trees, frames for drying
clothes, tethered goats and bird-cages at the foot of the Acropolis Socrates would still feel at home. Half-way up the long
approach folk art stalls, voluble women guides and sponge-
sellers with their netted loads bring back the present. Further up
still, over the steep stone-slab causeway there straggles a crocodile
of blue-smocked schoolchildren, a group of fat, corseted French-
women, camera-barnacled Germans, some Dutchmen in yachting
blazers and squat caps, an exquisite Indian girl in dark purple
sari, with entourage of chattering students. All struggle and pant
over the last big slabs and marble steps, about to flow over and
spoil, it would seem, the whole Acropolis. But once arrived they
are hushed, dwarfed, held still.

'There is an intoxication, a power of possession in its ruins and
the memories that inhabit them, which entirely prevents anyone
attempting to describe or estimate them,' wrote T. E. Lawrence.
In the brilliant thymy air, the bone-searching sunlight, we con-

front these monuments of classical Greece, infallible in their perfection, 'with the added beauty of the stains and hollows with which Time has endowed their stones'. The Parthenon, temple of the virgin Athena: the Erechtheum's caryatid porch of maidens; the small temple of Athena Nike, dominate this great hill effortlessly. A religious shrine from Homeric times, the Acropolis was rebuilt under Pericles, an intellectual aristocrat in power for thirty years, with the sculptor Phidias to direct and employ the leading talents of the whole Greek world. The values of that Athenian life shine out of the Pentelic marble still, through the Doric simplicity of the Parthenon and Propylaea, the Ionic grace and subtlety of Athena Nike and the later Erechtheum. They have the clarity, energy and unimpeded vision of Mediterranean sunlight. Every line of the mouldings, every refinement in the sculptures seems alive, perfect, inevitable in its place.

Below lie the Odeon, a Roman theatre and the Greek theatre of Dionysus; across there is the Hill of the Muses and Philopappos, favourite walk for courting couples, with a view to Aegina. On the other side the Areopagus, tribunal hill of Ares, the ancient Agora or market-place and the temple of Hephaestus. At the foot of the dark cliffs, whose height obliterates the noise from the city, there is a wild tumble of rooftops scrambling up the Acropolis base. And among the fallen granite and marble blocks on the plateau itself, shining crystalline in the sun, a blaze of brilliant red poppies, pink mesembryanthemum, deep yellow crown daisies, asphodel, mullein and purple thyme.

The obvious complement to the Acropolis is Mount Lykabettos. Between these two hills lies the heart of the city, the streets from Plateia Omonoia to Plateia Syntagma Here is the Mayfair of Athens: smart cafés like Floka and Zonar's, sumptuous hotels, the academy and the Zappeion. We made our way across this little London, a London with the traffic and the sunlight stepped up, with acacia and pepper instead of plane trees, to the secluded streets at the foot of Lykabettos, a rather un-Greek hill.

Zigzag paths and steps led up through prickly pear, dwarf pines and grey *Agave Americana* to the summit chapel of

St George. It was almost as rewarding as the Acropolis summit for viewpoint. A complete panorama of the city spread out below us—to Piraeus and Salamis where the Greeks had broken up the Persian invasion fleet of Xerxes in 480 BC, a panorama of white, sharp-cornered boxes, all with flat roofs, cubic penthouses and square boxes of chimneys, that extended up every surrounding hill. The small area of terra-cotta roofs of the old part seemed almost lost in their waves. From here the Field of Mars looked scarcely greener than the Sahara, the Zappeion a spider's web of paths and flower beds, the stadium a board for bagatelle; from the heart of the city miniature cars pumped out in endless streams. As the evening approached a cloudy-bronze sunset settled like a shield over the whole prospect and single golden rays lit up the cradle of western civilisation centred in it. 'No one could resist its spell. . . . I do not know how much was Athens and how much the colouring of my imagination upon it,' Lawrence admitted, 'I am coming back next year to stay a little time.'

From Thessaloniki, on course again, we head east, skirting lakes Koronia and Volvi, which almost cut off this region of Chalkidhiki from the mountains to the north. A reclaimed fertile plain surrounds us, with wheat and tobacco fields; there is cheerful colour in the villages—blue beehives, trees bordering the road painted in blue and white stripes, farms painted light or dark blue (Greek insistence on blue is as marked as the Indian's on pink), flowers in pots and, as backdrop, snow-covered peaks. In one of the fields an ass and an ox pull a plough.

Beyond the lakes—quite large and sea-like with yachting stations and a church built out at the end of a causeway—we enter the beautiful wooded valley of Stena Pendinas, the Macedonian Tempe. It provided a place of peripatetic study for perhaps the two most outstanding men who have ever met, the philosopher Aristotle and his pupil Alexander the Great. The road then hugs the shore, with sea not ten yards away and brown and black goats drinking from the shallow salty pools. We have it to ourselves apart from an occasional laden donkey. At the point where the river Struma runs down to the sea we find a strong bridge, brisk sentries and an impressive stone lion. Nearby, above the river bank, the remains of a once important city, Amphipolis, occupy the site of the ancient 'Nine Roads', a strategic point on the Via Ignatia.

After the wooded foothills of Mount Pangeon, a countryside of high villages, well-placed villas, well-kept vineyards, we take a 'tea-stop' at Eleutheroupolis. Its stony street ascends the hillside, a white donkey meanders up with panniers of manure, an old man totters down, negotiating the cobbles on two sticks. There are houses with neat flower gardens, bedding hung out of windows to air, hens scratching near kitchen doors. At the top a hard earth square screened by poplars gives on to the communal, white-washed well and tree-shaded church. Its wrought-iron gates, surmounted by a slender arch and wrought-iron crucifix, frame the roofs of the village and the sharp peaks that rise behind them. We look about at the white walls, the trellised vines, clean earth and crisp hills, savouring Greece. A lady all in black— headscarf, cardigan, apron, skirt, stockings, shoes—comes out to the well. Other women come out : children appear. The donkey, panniers empty and driver astride, is passing. He stops. We are asked in to the nearest house. It has two blue and two white walls, a tiled stove, chairs with red and yellow woven seats, a square-corner bed-settee with red-chequered coverlet, gay and clean. A girl brings us sugar cakes on saucers and cold water in red glasses : traditional hospitality. We are overwhelmed with courtesy and friendliness. The donkey driver has waited and insists on one of our girls taking his place to ride. So on the white donkey she, and we, return over the cobbles to the coach. Eleutheroupolis, you are remembered.

Within a few more miles, having climbed through a pass in the foothills we come upon Bob's 'best view in Macedonia'. A twisting descent through pine-woods angles sharply over the sea : there zooms into dramatic view a town piled up above its harbour, a splendid Roman aqueduct and a Byzantine castle, with a white church and high cross on the hill and the island of Thasos just beyond. The town is Kavalla, background to the film *Zorba the Greek* and as yet unspoiled. Down at the quayside we admire the night-fishing boats with their clusters of three pressure lamps astern, their bright nets (made in Japan) and blue, pink and orange floats. Climbing up through the narrow wynds and cobbled alleys to the old fortress, we view the eastern side of the town, the massive span of aqueduct and sleek bathing beaches. There is a lively market, back lanes of craftsmen's shops and a tangle of colourful streets in the older part. We eat at a glass-screened restaurant in the square—tender tentacles of squid, little pink fish fried in batter, moussaka and cauliflower in cheese sauce. Once called Neapolis, Christopolis in Byzantine times, Kavalla is the poor man's Monaco. Its 'Never-on-Sunday' atmosphere takes everyone's fancy. And only a few miles inland there is Philippi, where Brutus encountered Caesar's ghost and Greek drama is staged in the original theatre.

From Kavalla, taking one of the arches of the aqueduct, we pursue the surfy coastline of the Thracian Sea. A sloop sails into view on the turquoise water carrying the classic black sail. At a wayside market women stand chatting, in white kerchief headdresses, fringed lilac shoulder shawls and long grey, brown or slaty-blue dresses like the figures on an antique frieze. Beyond Xanthi, as we swing through the up-country villages and small towns, both men's and women's costume takes on a Turkish style. The women wear felt slippers, flowered cotton trousers, black bodices and shawls used to cover half their faces. Older men have the traditional wide black trousers, baggy in the crutch but tight at the knee, white knee-length stockings, black leather shoes, white cummerbunds and the red felt tarboosh. The houses are of mud brick enclosed behind continuous walls with a high door into the courtyard. Mosques and occasional minarets appear. Roadside shacks offer sausages and chestnuts, sauerkraut and sweetmeats kept hot over charcoal stoves. By the time we reach Alexandroupolis we feel we are already leaving Greece behind, although it is still 200 miles to Istanbul.

This last Greek night we spend within pebble-throw of the Aegean, setting up our tents in a fir clearing, with a cheerful fire of small branches and the company of frosty stars. We are lulled to sleep by the wash of the sea. It is a cool night and all are ready to rise early. We have our reward. Offshore 'rosy-fingered' dawn lights up the headland of Samothrace, the island on which was discovered the statue of Winged Victory.

After the frontier post at Kipi, scruffy on the Greek side, spacious and impressive—especially in military preparedness—on the Turkish, the countryside extends from wide, open ploughland and treeless slopes to a general brown bareness where the autoput rolls heavily up and down the heaves of terrain with Roman directness. The verges are gravel or sand, into which our coach was regularly forced by the thrusting passage of overloaded trucks heading west. There were glimpses of the turquoise Aegean, then of the grey-green or milky-aquamarine sea of Marmora. An occasional shepherd guarded his flock on this windswept countryside, ox teams were at work, burdened peasant women trudged along the side-roads. The one or two camping motels looked bleak and cheerless.

Tekirdag livened us up from our '*post Graecum triste*' mood. Its front aspect, full of pull-up cafés facing harbour installations, is uninviting, but a walk up to the market revealed a town of older manner and charm. Brown wooden two-storey houses with overhanging eaves in winding cobbled lanes—as in the Tudor towns of Cheshire—a fruit and fish market set under trees with silvery-blue fish arranged like the spokes of a wheel on large round, red trays, pyramids of oranges with their sprays of leaves, hanging baskets of mixed fruit, garlands of sausages on tree branches, boot-blacks with their elaborately decorated brass stands, all bosomy odalisques and coloured pin-ups—these spelt out the Turkish mode. Women in loose trousers and black half-veils, men in blue or yellow-bordered head gear, patriarchs in white to match their long white beards, upheld tradition. The garish Hollywood cinema posters forecast its future. Young girls showed the first signs : headscarfs, long pigtails and trousers for some, for others silk stockings, high heels, cigarettes and lipstick.

A dual carriageway soon decanted us from here to our third objective, Istanbul. In no time we were under a dust-and-soot charged sky, in a surge of grinning American cars, carts, taxis, buses and barrows, threading a hooter-infested way past traffic lights, point-duty men, milling pedestrians and porters, and down the ugly, ramshackle tramway-set street to Sultan Ahmet Square and the student hostel.

Istanbul, Stamboul, Constantinople, New Rome, Byzantium— by turn Turkish, French, Byzantine, Imperial Roman, Greek— 'depraved city of the damned', as vice-and-dope hunting journalists see it, has many faces and endless fascination : 'to see Constantinople is to see the entire East'. Its history and its situation (not excelled by Sydney or San Francisco) astride two continents and three seas encourage the active tourist to sample it in three sections, unless he is bamboozled into thinking that Sultan Ahmet Square and the buildings within a stone's throw, the Blue Mosque, the Church of the Holy Wisdom, Topkapi Palace and the underground palace cistern, constitute the cream of Istanbul touristique. South of the Golden Horn and extending up to the western land walls and 'Londra Asfalti' there is Istanbul proper. Then north of the Horn is Pera ('beyond'). On the Asian side of the Bosphorus lies Uskudar, known to admirers of Florence Nightingale as Scutari.

Pera, reached by Galata Bridge, goes back in tradition to the Genoese trading city of Galata on its southern slopes and is more European and Christian in character. Greeks settled there, trades of all kinds took root, French, Austrian, English communities developed. 'In Pera they speak Turkish, Greek, Hebrew, Armenian, Arabic, Persian, Russian, Sclavonian, Wallachian, German, Dutch, French, English, Italian, Hungarian,' remarked a traveller in 1717. In Galata itself the 'Turkification' is scarcely fifty years old and the sordid squatter areas in northern Pera indicate where Anatolian peasants were settled to accelerate the process. The other two sections of this great city of two million people share a generally Turkish and Islamic past.

Pera has the foreign embassies, travel agencies and principal shopping area, Istiklal Caddesi, formerly Grande Rue de Pera, and its Piccadilly, Taksim Square. An underground funicular, built by the French in 1873, hauls one up a quarter-mile of iron road from Galata bridge to shops where one can bespeak a hand-sewn suede coat and collect it within the day, for a mere 250TL.

Walking down again by the stepped and cobbled street past German bookshops, gramophone shops, printers', turnery and metalwork shops, junk stalls, flower-sellers and shellfish stalls, with now and again glimpses of the great circular Genoese watch-tower of Galata, one savours this area's special atmosphere. Cliffs of houses, black with age and neglect, crowd the alleys, their windows protected by heavy metal bars. Well-filled jeunes filles of the quarter lounge near the corner, a barber offers polyglot services; down some steps there is the entrance to an Italianate church; at the door of a jungly antique shop mother and daughter sit sipping tea and gossiping with the passers-by. Another village within a city.

In Istanbul proper everyone visits first the Blue Mosque of Sultan Ahmet. Compared with St Sophia, the Church of Holy Wisdom, built in the sixth century, Sultan Ahmet is not old or archetypal. But it combines a superb site and superb symmetry. The magnitude and delicacy, the grandeur and simplicity of its many domes and minarets, all gathered into a whole that soars towards heaven, constitute not so much a place of worship as an act of worship in itself.

As we cast our shoes and dipped through the heavy leather entrance curtain our first sight was of a worshipper in long grey caftan and emerald green head-dress kneeling on a red carpet near a sunny window niche, to face Mecca as he read the Koran aloud, while pigeons primly strutted in the bars of sunlight and the radiance reflected from the dome. Columns of white marble and malachite, windows of gentian blue, sea-green, orange, crimson and pearly white created pools of subdued colour without distracting from the misty bluebell haze in which the whole interior surface of galleries, balconies, upper columns and great dome seem suspended. The eye can rarely detect which surfaces are of blue ceramic tiles and which of blue stencilling. The only incongruous element in the huge, carpeted blue-lit cavern of the interior is a low overhead network of wires, like a miniature railway track, that carries the electric lights—and the two London-made grandfather clocks fitted into marble niches. . . .

We emerge through the knot of postcard-sellers, shoeshine

boys, boys hawking rings of nutty bread on sticks, clinging guides and hissing money-changers to walk to the covered market, Kapali Carci. Once inside we are engulfed. Not only among its ninety-two arched passages and its four thousand covered stalls, but by the thrusting crowds, the harsh glitter of lights, the microphone-reinforced battery of sales-jack appeals.

Among the chief bazaars of the Near East, Cairo, Aleppo, Constantinople, this was always regarded as the finest until Ankara became Turkey's seat of government and the old capital of Empire was reduced to provincial status. The inner market, devoted to stones, gold and silver, ivory, jade, ikons, brass, copper, enamels, meerschaum etc, surrounds its valuable pieces with as much gimcrack as most bazaars. In the haphazardly piled stalls can be found relics of every cultural tide—Phoenician, Greek, Persian, Arabic, Roman—that has flowed in and around the Mediterranean. The open streets of the outer fringe offer incredibly scruffy heaps of old toothbrushes, bootbrushes, bottles, plastic boxes, cosmetic jars, pots, pans, old knives, bits of rusty metal, screws, buttons, watch parts, spectacle lenses set out on the muddy cobblestones among the cat-scavenged refuse. Who on earth buys this junk? Under filthy sagging awnings tattered old men sit dazed and crumpled over tiny charcoal stoves, shapeless women in shawls and yashmaks wheeze and waddle, rag-sorters jostle and scuffle and, in odd corners, on piles of mildewed books with newspapers for blanket, the derelicts, paralytics, helpless amputees withdraw into their personal miasma, squeezed up like grotesque netsukes.

The main passageways, of course, are really the streets of various trades, furriers, quilt-makers, cloak-makers, cloth-sellers, furnishers, carpet-sellers, grocers, hardware dealers, slipper-sellers where both town and country come for everyday needs. These packed alleyways shout with garish colour—columns spirally papered with Turkish glamour-girl postcards, whole walls of aniline-dyed carpet or acid-hued brocade—and release a flood tide of gew-gaws in plastic and cheap Japanese goods. Then there is the Arabian Nights' spice-market, an esoteric world of its own.

Leaving Kapali Carci by one of the outside lanes where grunt-
ing Armenian porters ('hamal') struggled to carry on their leather-
padded backs gas stoves and refrigerators, iron bedsteads and
spin-dryers or huge bales of cloth, with headbands straining at
their neck muscles, sweat dripping and eyes always on their feet,
we passed under an arch to enter the almost magical opposite to
bazaar clamour. The large flag-stoned court here hidden behind
a mosque, shaded by trees and vines, contains all or nearly all the
city's second-hand bookshops. There are illuminated Korans and
Rubáiyáts, French romances and Byronic novelettes in Turkish,
text-books and German manuals, popular science and sex magazines and the usual detritus of English and American fiction.
Students and scholars, coming to browse in this oasis for an hour,
lose themselves for half a day. Even the band of an approaching
anti-Communist procession failed to disturb them.

The best way to see the Golden Horn is by water, on one of the
ferry-boats which ply a zigzag course from shore to shore up to
waterhead at Eyup. After a Galata speciality, a fish sandwiched
in a bread roll, caught, cooked and thrown to the customer from
one of the small boats moored beside the bridge, we walked over
to No 6 landing. A ferry promptly backed in, the waiting crowd
surged and elbowed forward and with a 'Whoop-Whoop-
Whoooop' and belch of black smoke we were off.

The sail to Eyup which lasts forty minutes, offers the basic
Istanbul scenes. A skyline of vast soap-bubble mosques; boatyards
with half-stripped tramps, barnacled hulks so old that they might
be 'quinqueremes of Nineveh', bobbing sloops and naval cutters
from the Admiralty dockyard (the bridge opens at night for
larger ships to pass through); urchins drifting or splashing oars
downstream; the powerful thrust of Galata Tower and the ugly
yellow-walled cement works, warehouses, slaughter-houses and
old and crumbling wooden 'yali' or waterside houses. This is the
underbelly of a Golden Horn which appears now as a sewer, a
sump of floating vegetable waste at the foot of seven slag-heaps,
now as the gilded necklace of the Seven Hills of Byzantium,
according to conditions. Like the dust-and-soot-laden sky, sud-

denly cleared to brilliance in spring by the icy wind ('poyros') from the Black Sea, or in autumn by 'lodos' the south wind, the whole waterway can be transfigured by a change of light beneath the beholder's fascinated eye.

It was at Eyup that the exotic novelist and Turcophil, Louis-Marie-Julien Viaud, officer in the French navy, nom-de-plume Loti, had his house for rendezvous and 'rahat'—that retreat from life into voluptuous nothingness and drifting oriental dream, known to Arabs as 'kif'. Dressed in baggy trousers, gold-embroidered jacket and fez, he would sit under the plane tree, smoking a tchibouk, to gaze out over the windings of the Golden Horn and the cypress-pointed cemetery, at sunset. In the Loti Kahvesi some of his household effects remain: embroidered cushions, a green-tiled porcelain stove, wall ottomans, oriental rugs, tables inlaid with mother-of-pearl, copper bowls, narghiles, between the walls and ceilings of varnished bamboo. A charming girl in traditional Turkish costume serves tea in the warm air of scented geraniums and a quiet stirred only by the gentle hiss of the samovar. Rahat. . . .

The graveyards of Istanbul, havens of quiet or picnic spots by day, resorts of prostitutes by night, substitutes for gardens in the vicinity of markets, cafés and cab ranks, are in themselves rare gardens flowering in marble and stone. The one below Loti's café near the mosque is rivalled only by the great cemetery of Uskudar. Slender columns crowned with garland, fez or intricately wound Bey's turban, rise like tulips among the grasses in ranks and clusters: graceful upright slabs, diagonally inscribed with lettering, verses from the Koran, emblematic lilies or Turkish crescents and arabesques lean towards the wall grilles or stand aloofly upright. They accompany one down to the mosque courtyard, where one is greeted by a clattering upheaval of pigeons and wary looks from the bedraggled resident storks. There are stalls of framed calligraphic texts, scenes from the life of the Prophet, stalls of beads and prayer caps: grey-beards perform ritualistic ablutions at taps in stone troughs, country women in bundly black, and pale swollen girls with dark eyes file past. It is a place of pilgrimage and ardent devotion, with the tomb of

Mohammed's standard bearer, to which Turks and Moslems come to pray from far afield.

We too filed past the outer wall, panelled with delicate blue tiles of every age and pattern, past the finely wrought copper grille 'the Window of Need', worn shiny by the lips and fingers of the devout, and briefly entered the tomb. The sarcophagus behind its grille, the glowing colours of tiles and faience, the richly patterned carpet and numerous dim lamps, the murmured prayers of the pilgrims, harmonised mystical beauty and miraculous faith. The main entrance to the mosque stood across the courtyard. We passed under the leather curtain to be confronted by a sea of shiny trouser seats. Service was in progress and while the Imam chanted verses from the Koran hundreds of men in cotton prayer-caps knelt and touched their foreheads to the ground. The interior of this mosque is small, light and clear, with pearly white marble pillars, plain stone walls, no tiles or coloured glass but a fine blue-green carpet covering the whole floor.

So by the stone-flagged lane through more thickets of tombstones and back to the ferry landing. Arrived at Galata Bridge we lingered and looked back. Against a dust-refulgent haze, golden, peach, then deepening to purple, the great mosques, minarets, and belvederes of the palace cut black silhouettes, while the Golden Horn was flooded with saffron-yellow. Gradually the maimed beggars, the staggering porters and bustling tugs faded from sight and a moon of eastern splendour rose over Asia like some impossibly large, lop-sided orange balloon.

Three days, a week, a month are as nothing for the exploration of Istanbul. Its noise, dust, dilapidation, squalor first repel, then challenge : with such hidden relics as the 'Hans' or Byzantine inns, massive as fortresses, for camel trains, merchants and their goods, near the bazaar (still in use as workshops); or the floral-tiled mosque of Sokollu Mehmet Pasa with its revolving marble pillar, used in earthquakes to test for shifts of the structure. Finally it mesmerises. There are so many individual quarters : Cagologlu on the second hill with Ankara Caddesi twisting down towards the Horn, like Fleet Street and Charing Cross combined;

Page 71: (left) A gate-
way at Persepolis; (right)
tribeswoman of Yazd,
Iran

Page 72: (*left*) At Amol on the Caspian coast; (*below*) Goochan in northern Iran

the theatrical and almost vertical streets behind Sulimanye mosque that lead towards Seven Towers and the sea wall, all cobbled in overlapping hoop patterns, shaded by acacia trees, scavenged by grey, white and marmalade cats, overhung by bleached, greyish wooden houses with closely-grilled upper storeys their pavements crowded with tea-benches and fruit-stalls. They remind one of stage scenery, fronts with nothing behind. Again there is the promenade beyond Yenakapi and its shaded 'gazinos', its fairground and road tunnel under the railway with even shadier shops. Or Topkapi Palace and Seraglio with its complex of mysterious pavilions and incredibly opulent and ostentatious collection of Sultans' treasures, from Ming and Sung porcelain to a 66-carat diamond solitaire and Meissen tea-bowls smothered in emeralds. Or the belly-dance dives of Galata . . .

Somewhat dazed after our dip into this 'paradise for pimps and pariahs, all peacock tiles and choked drains', we emerged early on the fourth morning through a barrage of police whistles, hooting buses, blaring radios, screaming 'dolmus' (shared taxis), shouting vendors, bulbous Dodges, rattling carts and echoing ships' sirens on to Londra Asfalti. (Those coming through Vienna, Belgrade, Sofia join in here.)

Again we back-tracked westward, at first, along the deep blue sea of Marmora, past Silivri and Tekirdag, and headed for Kesan and Gallipoli. Of the two ways of entering Asia, by car ferry from Galata to Uskudar, or by the more chancy ferry from the Gallipoli peninsula to Canakkale, the latter was chosen. (For Ankara, of course, and places forward to Syria or for the Black Sea Coast route to Trebizond for Iran, the Uskudar ferry serves best.) Kesan is an everyday, picturesque country town. Its cobbled square and lilac-painted shops, uncertain whether closed or open and none well-stocked, its old black and red barouches, the sausages hanging from tree branches, the baggy-trousered women scrubbing carpets at the well, the old lady in black driving a two-ox waggon up the main street, the schoolchildren in peaked caps and stiff white Eton collars, might all have come out of a Turgenev novel. As the coach eased cautiously over the bumps

E

and hollows a family of tinkers lashed their pony trap to pass, sitting fur-hatted, soot-black among a medley of copper vessels. Villages and towns like this, in their wide plain of palisaded farms, sunflower and cornfields, devious roads and fierce dogs, account for eighty per cent of the Turkish population: men of the fields, peasants, far off in outlook, material comfort, economic progress from the men of the cities.

We coasted along, in and out of bays, through Galata village to the busy muddled little quayside of Eceabat. We chose for camp a level stretch of turf near a clear spring running into an old stone basin. There was a live turtle in the adjacent pool, a spreading mulberry tree and soon the crackle and flare of a drift-wood fire on the shingle. Foraging among the rockpools someone came up with a panful of small crabs. The stoves burned steadily in the calm air, the sea took on an opalescent sheen, occasional bats thinly twanged, the sky turned apricot-plum again and in the gathering dusk we supped, facing the Asian shore.

Crossing this short stretch of water the next morning had an exhilaration of its own—quite different from a Channel crossing. We were casting away from the known to the completely un-known. Would the coach make it now, all that long, arduous, uncertain road across Asia Minor to the other side of India and Nepal? Would we find ourselves stranded somewhere, be caught up in some epidemic, wilt in the coming heats or simply lose our mutual tolerance? The new coastline seemed an opening chal-lenge, the sparkling strait a Rubicon. We toasted the enterprise in glasses of purple syrup bought from the itinerant drink-seller aboard and did not look back.

# 3  IN ASIA MINOR

*Only the Oriental knows how to live inwardly, within himself, his home.*

Pierre Loti

Canakkale greeted us with the first cab in Asia, two-horse, red-canopied, gilt-fringed, open-seated, lamp-lit, solid-tyred and heavily sprung. The smiling, dark, shirt-sleeved cabby, with his pointed heel-trodden shoes, seemed confident of its excellence as a mode of transport. In Asia the old accompanies the new until it wears out—or even longer.

We took the road to Troy, a distance of barely thirty kilometres, among the foothills of Mount Ida, but with the twists and changes of direction, the obstructing farms and farmyard traffic, it felt as many miles.

> Troops of unattended horses; here and there
> Some little hamlets, with new names uncouth,
> Some shepherds (unlike Paris) led to stare
> A moment at the European youth,
> Whom to the spot their schoolboy feelings bear.

Byron's lines still apply: the ways are country-quiet, inconspicuously signed, as unremarkable as Lincolnshire lanes. Then at the end of a long monotonous stretch there suddenly appears a modern restaurant, a cluster of curio shops, a small museum, a park.

The Trojan horse is displayed everywhere, in Disney contours, on postcards, badges, wine bottles, amphorae, plaques, woven bags, swinging signs, together with the heroes in Technicolor

75

scenes of action. 'Where I sought for Ilion's walls. The quiet sheep feeds and the tortoise crawls', is a thing of the past. Package tours and their amenities have seen to that.

The remains of the eight or nine cities now brought to light exercise a powerful magnetism. Granite blocks from pre-Homeric times, great stone monoliths forming gateposts and lintels, deep defensive entrance ways, half-buried house lineaments, the tremendous outer defences and the broken marble columns, speak a language that Hector and Achilles knew, in the same 'vast, untilled and mountain-skirted plain' of rustling grass and asphodel that stretches away from the Hellespont to the Aegean. A solitary thorn bush leans from the walls towards the hillock of their tombs. In the museum are the relics from the excavations—clay oil lamps, delicate figurines, miniature heads from one to only one-third of an inch high, models of doves and tortoises, an exquisite group of a woman feeding a child, various black-patterned terra-cotta vessels, glass bottles and looped and twisted glass stirrers, as well as hero-sized statuary. Troy, they remind us, had been a place of settlement since 2500 BC.

We gaze our fill across Scamander's windy plain 'where a hundred thousand men might fight again with ease', then push on, southward. The road flings its hairpin bends over hill and gorge country of pinewoods smelling of dust and incense. Shepherds in white turbans and white fleecy coats sit in the turfy clearings cross-legged among their flocks of new black and white lambs. Later, as we skirt the eastern shores of the Aegean, the dim blue outlines of a multitude of islands come into view and on the other side, beyond fringes of tall feathery reeds, lights in hill villages twinkle through the gathering dusk. At Edremit we descend on a modest hotel : tiny rooms, 4TL each, with two beds and only windows opening into a corridor, screened by lattice : a single cold-water basin in a dark corner on each floor.

Camel trains were being loaded on the coastal road that took us from Edremit to Bergama (Pergamum). With their orange flank-cloths, wooden saddle-frames and pendent bells above heavy splay feet and horny knees, they regarded the proceedings with an air of weary superciliousness, broken only by an occasional rictus that displayed great caggy teeth and purple gums. A sheep market was being held at Bergama, fat-tailed rams ambled down the road, their fleeces dyed yellow or orange, blue or red ribbons tied at their rumps and in some cases gilded horns. A two-man band paraded the rambling, cobbled streets, wearing bells at knee and wrist and parti-coloured waistcoats. Among the pleasant shady alleys saddle-making, donkey-shoeing, cloak-making, bread-baking and barbering were in progress; from each open shop issued a smell of leather, wax, horn, wool, meal, singed hair and bay-rum. Coppersmiths beat a cheerful tattoo in answer to the staccato tap of shoe-makers' hammers. An old white-washed courtyard in a side-street had a Romanesque arch and part of a Corinthian column built into the entry.

From the old acropolis, to which we climbed by grassy slopes bright with red anemones, Bergama presents as picturesque an appearance as any town of its size in Turkey. The old city with its excavated brick buildings, temples, narrow streets and gymnasium of Greek and Roman times looks down on the only less old of ruined towers, a worn stone bridge over a green-foaming river, huge brick basilica, slender minarets and colour-washed pantiled houses. The streets are full of character: private doors have hand-shaped brass knockers, a church door one of lyre shape; the shops are painted lilac, pale blue, cream, pale green; there is a newish market hall in gay, cinema-style décor and a street market, past which faytons speed with a tinkle of bells and flash of polished brass headlamps.

After an afternoon by wide and sparkling bays, with glimpses of Lesbos and smaller islands, we became gradually engulfed in the blocks of new flats, the sidings and shipyards, the tatty market streets, broad boulevards and 'sexational' cinemas that make up modern Izmir, ancient Smyrna. The city where Tantalus died and Antigonus Cyclops had his capital, where Byron finished the first draft of *Childe Harold* and the author of *Fanny Hill* spent his early manhood as British Consul, is about the size of Leeds. It extends in a long row of indifferent buildings along the Karachikaya embankment, broken half-way by a tortuous narrow street choked with stalls, hucksters, marketing Turks and megaphone touts.

But just beyond the wide curve of Izmir's bay a Kervansaray
Mocamp provided a pleasant overnight. These camps have been
established in the principal tourist areas of Turkey under the
aegis of BP and for 7.50TL we pitched tents under orchard trees
with the amenities of a kitchen, shop, bar, washrooms and peace.

From Izmir to Ephesus the carefully tended countryside mixed
bold natural features with the bright details of spring, almond-
blossom, asphodel and anemones bordering a green and purple
plain in a frame of impressive hills. Another market day was in
progress at Selcuk where palms shaded the streets and storks'
nests crowned the chimneys. Women in pink, white and grey-
checked cotton head-shawl or white head-dress falling to the
shoulders, and full black skirts, crowded stalls selling goats'-milk
cheese in skins, murderous-looking clasp knives, brightly painted
wooden spoons, floral shirts, shawl lengths and piles of vegetables
and fruit. Against the dark hillside the blue and white pencil of
a minaret streaked skywards. Everyone was friendly, offering us
sunflower seeds or nuts to chew.

The streets of the upper town are especially photogenic—blue
houses, rosy pantiles, courtyard walls and iron balconies carrying
pots of geranium, begonia and basil, dark brown donkeys
tethered against brilliant, smooth white walls or beside carved
old wooden doors and feathery acacia trees. The shops offer egg-
shaped hand-rollers of onyx or alabaster and those hypnotic blue
beads like eyes—designed to keep off the evil eye.

Ephesus is only a few kilometres down the road, the site from
whose early excavation Mark Twain's party carried off 'fragments of sculptured marbles and ornaments broken from the
interior work of mosques', which they were made to disgorge at
Smyrna. A complete town has now been revealed in this fold of
the bare hills: market place, theatre to seat 35,000, library,
brothels with frescoes and tesselated floor, long, paved and colonnaded streets, temples and harbour road, all in fine golden stone
or honey-coloured marble. Some of the arches at the gates rest
upon piers fifteen feet square of solid masonry, not shafts filled
with rubble. The friezes and statuary, torsos and heads, horses
and elephants in the keystones of arches have a fresh, living

quality in the brilliant light. There are inscribed tablets in the streets setting out laws and regulations. Fragments of sandy-blue Roman glass lie about in odd corners.

Ephesus, once proudest city of the ancient world, seat of the Temple of Diana—one of the world's seven wonders, the place from which Rome administered the whole province of Asia, known to the feet of Alexander, of Hannibal, Anthony, the Apostle Paul, Mary Magdalen, the Crusaders, owed its downfall as much to the silting up of its harbour and the ravages of malaria as to the spoliation of the Goths. Now only marshes and a few cottages remain by the sea. The Temple of Diana is open to the winds : her effigy, that of a many-breasted fertile goddess, divine mother linked in some myths with the symbol of the Queen of the Bees, stands now in the little museum at Selcuk, mysteriously glowing in translucent honey-coloured marble. But the genius loci of Ephesus remains, as strong as ever.

Through the gorge spanned by its Roman aqueduct we came out beyond Selcuk into the river plain of the Menderes, whose windings explain the word 'meander'. The countryside up to Aydin rivals that of the Ticino in northern Italy for its avenues of Lombardy poplars, its orange groves and meadows of anemones, its bosky hills, ochre-coloured rock, deep watercourses and distant snow-capped mountains. There are blue farmsteads among fields of white daisies, where sheep carcases hang up in the yards for skinning. Gipsy encampments add their flashes of hectic colour. Storks comb the ditches for frogs, their red bills, orange legs, fine black and white feathers shining in the sun. In summer all would be olives, vineyards, opium poppy and sunflower fields.

Aydin, situated off the main highway on a gentle slope with spacious squares, is a town of unadvertised, unspoiled charm. Its open-air cafés, orderly bazaar, fine mosque with fluted minarets deserved a day—or at least a night : Denizli—closed for siesta—did not. We passed through both and on to the hot springs of Pammukale, pitching tents for protection against a tearing wind in the lee of massive Roman walls.

Anatolia's claim to richness of historical associations and diversity of natural scenery—and each of Turkey's four coastal regions, Mediterranean, Aegean, Marmora and Black Sea, has its own distinctive character—is well sustained by Pammukale, which lies on a plateau a few kilometres off the Denizli—Dinar road. From the mineral hot springs (93F), converted into a bathing-pool-with-restaurant, the stream of steaming water flows down over a series of limestone cascades just below the road, with shallow blue pools and terraces spread out in a wide natural arc like so many water-lily leaves, the rock shining crystalline white. Individual cascades, formed by the lime deposits, are up to four or five times man-height and fringed with stalactites. Despite their appearance of slippery ice it is easy to scramble down from level to level, with one's feet in warm water, basking in the strongly reflected sun.

Waking at Pammukale, after a stormy night of flapping tents and sorties to pile boulders on the guy ropes, was to re-enter an older world. Among the rocks and fragments of wall a shepherd and shepherd boy watched immobile as their flock grazed the close turf : they wore stiff coats of white felt with wing-like sleeves and close-fitting conical caps. Giant yellowy-green euphorbia grew on the margin of the Roman watercourse. Above, jutting against a Mediterranean blue sky, rose the stone tiers of a classical theatre. The worn stone seats were comfortable, the details of acanthus pattern on the Corinthian columns, of the rose and of the egg and knife, symbols of life and death, carved on the marble blocks, was still sharp. Broken columns showed the method of their erection, with a central pin between courses and channel for pouring in molten lead to seal the join, while the position of blocks could be adjusted by means of copper wedges. A large fragment of statuary had the finely modelled torso of a young man holding a leafy branch, his discarded robe folded away over one shoulder; another was seated in the lap of a robed female under the shade of a fruit tree.

Apart from its warm pool and frozen falls and its theatre Pammukale has an octagonal early Christian church and a long empty avenue of tombs. Here are six-berth sarcophagi in which whole families were laid, parents on the upper stone shelves, their children on the lower. One walks between them and the vast stone coffins mounted on plinths expecting some manifestation, as at a raree show. All we saw were two workmen from the 'diggings' with a pocket full of Greek, Roman and Crusader bronze and silver coins to sell. . . .

From Pammukale to Antalya the road takes one into the 'lake district' of this region. The Menderes' windings have produced a series of ox-bow lakes in addition to the two sheets of water named on the map. Thick muddy, chocolate-brown streams, after the night's storm, coursed down the hills and over the low-lying fields, making the road quite turbulent. The ascent towards Burdur by a series of hairpin bends gave striking views of an unusual lake, beautifully coloured in tones ranging through pale, greeny-blue to aquamarine and barred with broad ribs of sand well out from the shore. A small steam train, engine in reverse, chugged across by the lakeside and children held out water lily buds.

From the high point, at about 4,000ft, we came down from hill and lake country into the palm-dotted, orange-grove plain that meets the sea at Antalya. The town and its situation are delightful in spring; one sunbathes at Christmas, bathes by February. A tall brick tower—the 'grooved minaret'—dominates the town centre; around it and in a beehive-roofed museum treasures of classical sculptures are assembled. Below this a huddle of brown pantiled roofs, punctuated by cypresses, spreads down to the boat-jostling harbour and across the gulf, as backdrop the Lycian Taurus extends in sharply-cut snow-capped peaks. The streets of the town, especially the wide, tree-lined promenade leading to the park, are filled with tinkling faytons, their horses tossing bright red tassels and pom-poms. People stroll along vine-trellised walks or sip their coffee on balconies in the warm evening sun. At nightfall the Taurus carves a dramatic black silhouette against a sky of deep peacock blue. In season this ancient town is now a booming tourist resort.

After one night in Antalya we drove along the sea-bitten coast road with repeated climbs and descents to green land-of-Canaan plains, past Serik and Side, a ruined city with a huge amphitheatre in a Piranesian state of decay. Whips of rain flicked across the coach windows, blurring the banana plantations, terraces of tillage and goatherds' mud hovels. There were wild lilies and purple daphne in the woods, magpies and wagtails among the débris of choked watercourses. Great mountains appeared to the north—the Taurus main range—and on the other side unchanging blue-green sea.

Alanya is attractive even in the rain : it is built on two conical hills, with modern villas below the escarpment, palms and graceful minarets profiled by the slope. At Anamur we took our lunch at an 'ordinary'—stewed mutton, beans, potatoes, stuffed peppers, tomatoes, with bread, borsk (cheese pasty) or yoghourt, and coffee—Turkish in style, cheap and expeditiously served for 6TL each. At Selifke a river had flooded and houses stood in two feet of water. Small boats rocked on the turgid, chocolate-brown current, shops were isolated in lagoons and people waded knee-deep to their homes. It was a Riviera landscape under mistral conditions, instead of the soft airs and sapping humidity of late spring or early summer. Our vision of coralline rocks and crystalline pools for bathing gave place to notions of securing a comfortable night. From the wooden rooms of a chalet motel whose shutters and doors banged and lights failed, while a praying mantis hibernated undisturbed, we watched sand whipped across the shore by a north wind and the sun set in stormy brilliance, giving a *son et lumière* effect to the old fort out to sea.

'Heaven' and 'hell'—Cennet and Cehennem as they appear on the map—came next day. A huge cave has been formed, either by meteorite or water erosion, like a collapsed, convex pot-hole. Its quarry-type approach leads, by 450 steps, to a dark subterranean passage with a stream which eventually runs out to sea. Plants hang from the vertical walls, stalactites drip coldly, finally all light from the sky is lost in abysmal gloom. Near the bottom are the ruins of a small church—representing Heaven. Tradition has it that prisoners were held in the lowest part of the cave and after trial either gave thanks for their release, in the church, or if found guilty, were thrown down from the cliff into Hell. The whole place possessed a suggestive awe even at 8 am.

The coast road to Mersin, a clean, busy, naval port, led through banana plantations, olive, orange and lemon groves. The sea was bright blue, the sun warm again : in a few weeks the gardens here would be smothered in morning glory, hibiscus, oleanders and camellias, the fields filled with huge tomatoes, maize and sunflowers. Mersin is a civilised town, with many jewellers specialising in filigree silverwork and a range of European magazines in the news-stands. It would make an excellent jumping off place for exploration of south-east Anatolia, instead of the 'cottonopolis' of inland Adana which has a livelier atmosphere but becomes a steaming bowl on warm nights. (Adana itself and Antakya [Antioch] are usually staging posts for travellers forward to Syria, the Lebanon, Jordan and Iraq.)

At Tarsus, entered by Cleopatra's Gate—she sailed up the Cydnus dressed as Aphrodite to meet Anthony here—we turned our backs on the Mediterranean at last and began to snuff the more invigorating air of the Taurus. The majestic corridor through these mountains, the Cilician Gates by which Alexander's armies passed to defeat Darius the Persian in the plain of Issus near Adana, reaches an altitude of 4,300ft and is of great length and splendour. Soon the coach was negotiating an endless series of tortuous bends and punishing gradients : the rocky, ice-green watercourses, great conifers, the sharp air, chalet dwellings and the shining snow plumes blown from the peaks heralded another sort of Anatolia. At the upper end of the long, complex valley, with its side gorges, projecting limestone pinnacles, narrow 'necks', its cliffs fissured with snow, magnificent climbing buttresses and sun-glittering icy peaks, a high plateau opens on an Alpine pastoral scene. Donkeys graze under willows, Turkoman nomads sit round an open fire in an encampment of sack-cloth or black goats-hair tents : there is a locanta for truck drivers with green benches and rush-bottomed chairs on the veranda; a foaming white stream from the upper slopes runs alongside the road.

As we cross the plateau and look down towards Pozanti real Shangri-la is revealed. Chalets with wide eaves and blue-grey roofs, trim gardens behind low walls of rounded stones spread up among the firs and larches almost to the snow line : heather and pink saxifrage colour the nearer slopes, black lambs frisk about and a handsome red-brown-and-white bird, like a cock pheasant, struts by the stream. Secluded in their valley head, with Toros Degi towering over 11,000ft out of the snowfield above, these chalet-dwellings give a foretaste of the Himalayan villages of Nepal.

From Pozanti and its wild-west looking railway and film-set locomotives, the road forward to Nigde stays high, reaching 5,000ft at one point, and crosses a wide, treeless, snow-bound plateau with the Taurus or anti-Taurus ranges always in view. We startled a mountain fox, lost count of the ditched or over-turned trucks and passed what looked like a peasant wedding procession. Gaily dressed women filled a first cart, men the two following : a red banner on a pole signalised their mission.

In the 'Dr Zhivago' countryside beyond Nigde, bare, rock-strewn, crossed by an earth road between ragged poplars, we came into view of Erciyas Dagi or Mt Argaeus. This queen of mountains, a beautifully shaped mass over 13,000ft with fine long ridge and sharp double peak, changed as we skirted its base and frozen lake, from glittering white to matt cream, from rich gold to old rose and finally to lilac in the shadowed light at sun-down. Suddenly, out of nowhere, ten large aluminium silos or storage tanks rose up ahead. Before we were close enough to identify them a rough side road swung up from the plateau into the hills. We climbed, now between banks of snow, to the top and a last violet glimpse of the 'Queen', then were swinging down in tortuous twists through blank-eyed villages to a narrow valley. It began to look like the road to nowhere until, suddenly again, a rocky mass rose up on the left with lights twinkling in it. Our long day—370km in testing terrain—ended at Urgup, 'a desert place which you might think was outside this earth'.

A remarkable place even for this remarkable country, Urgup is a semi-troglodyte town piled up against a gleaming white tufa cliff. The cliff walls are veined with streaks of yellow and pink, there are occasional glimpses of orchards and vineyards, other-wise the whole agglomeration of dwellings and rock seems one mass of dazzling chalk. Looking up the main street towards the square and the mosque, whitely brilliant above, one had the illusion that they might all melt back into the cliff with the melting of the snow that covered them. The cliff itself is honeycombed with hundreds of dwelling-places, oratories, wine-cellars, granaries half in use, half in decay. The porous rock has made cutting and carving easy. Some of the houses are quite modern, with wooden porches to an entrance cave at the cliff foot, a passage to stables and storehouse, then a flight of steps leading up to the dwelling-rooms excavated in the cliff face, provided with windows in front. There are ornamental gateways opening on to dovecote-like cells, false windows, niches of all sizes and blank stairways. Schoolgirls in black smocks and white collars were running down the twisting alleys between these fretted eyries. Above them, there stand, outlined against blue sky, great cones of rock, forty to a hundred feet high, crowned with the disk-shaped caps of harder rock which have been the cause both of their formation and preservation; these also were honeycombed with doorways, chambers and window openings.

The landscape beyond is of soft volcanic rock, covered originally by hard stratum, which has led to the formation of a whole forest of caves among the pinnacles, pyramids, needles, cones and jutting dragon's teeth, which extend to terraced cliffs and escarpments on the greyish-white horizon. In the ravine of Goreme, a concealed petrified valley to the left of the road, communities of Christian monks of the old Cappadocian race sought refuge from Arab, Turk and Mongol between the third and eighth centuries. They hollowed out not only their scarcely accessible cells, but also extraordinary chapels, crypts and oratories, some of which can only be entered by pigeon-loft steps or by slithering through a tunnel. Within the fantastic chimneys, the pumice cones and pyramids with their precarious stone caps one finds colonnades carved from solid rock, tables and benches, wine-presses and lamp niches and kitchens. Deep in the gloom there is a complete church with holy pictures on the crumbling walls and gilded Byzantine frescoes. A Maltese cross, an open eye gazing from the roof, patterns of small animals gradually become visible. There are many such churches, ghostly cathedrals completely withdrawn from the world. In one, the 'Dark Church', the birth of Christ, the figures of Lazarus and Judas, the Last Supper, Palm Sunday and the Crucifixion are all preserved in fine colour and remarkable facial expression. This world within a world becomes almost more real than the one outside, until from a high balcony within the rock one looks out to all the other immuring pinnacles, their bases so close that they touch each other, thrusting up from the ravine floor towards the plateau and the sun.

Continuing across this 'moonscape' past the villages of Machan and Ujissa and another great rocky outcrop of troglodyte dwellings jutting up from the plateau like some feature of the Colorado desert, we found Nevsehir, a rougher town than Urgup, piled in a medley of white and yellow cube-shaped houses and minarets against a snow-streaked hillside. Then on to the final bizarre monument of this region. 'Underground city, underground city' chanted the muddy little boys and little girls with bootlace pigtails as the coach edged into a rough square between high walls. A whole posse of bright-aproned young women, covering their mouths and eyes, their plaited hair ornamented with silver coins and cowrie shells stood at gaze while a bearded elder led us to the 'city' entrance. Built by the Hittites three thousand years ago it was a refuge for 30,000 people. Numerous steps and inclines led down under the hill, here at about 4,500ft, and into the uppermost of a seven-storey warren of subterranean chambers, linked by passages usually wide enough to admit a horse and capable of being closed off by large solid disks of stone. The light of a Tilley lamp showed us large chambers, some with bins for grain and mangers, smaller low-roofed family rooms, wells and winepresses and a church. Their extent seemed interminable and all were kept fresh by air shafts. The living areas were used by early Christians during times of persecution and from this city tunnels were said to have been constructed to Goreme. . . . As we returned there across the lunar plateau sunset suffused the distant porphyritic peaks of Mt Argaeus with a deep pink glow and the isolated outcrop town stood dark against the frosty sky.

Next morning the MCW would not start. The reason soon became obvious: the bite in the air at 7 am was breath-catching. Thawing out and warming up the engine took an hour—until the sun moved round to the coach.

The road now ran between levels of glistening, satin-textured snow to Kayseri (Caesarea), an important trade centre, historically, on the Roman highway from Ephesus to the Euphrates. Its old castle, built on the foundations of the Emperor Justinian's fortress, has large picturesque towers flanked by the Seljuk lion in bold relief. From there seemingly endless highlands, the northern fringe of the anti-Taurus range, take the road up to 6,000ft between peaks of 9,000ft on the long drive to Gurun. At a typical kahveh, on the wooden balcony overhanging the stream that courses between muddy banks through the middle of the town, we watched Army troopers cantering down to water their brown ponies. Blue-eyed men in wide breeches and bala-clavas of double thickness, teased brown wool worked in zigzag patterns, struck virile attitudes and a fat fruitstall-holder proudly displayed for us the longest moustaches in Turkey—curved down to his chin and then looped up behind each ear. The place has a wild, brigandish air with its honeycomb of rock houses in the cliffs behind and a wildly beautiful gorge where a tributary of the Euphrates comes down.

The folds and dips and great swinging waves in this now completely snow-bound highland of central Anatolia—the edge of that great western plain which from the air in summer seems one unbroken, barbaric mixture of red and brown soil and convulsed rock—took us between banked verges sometimes as high as the coach. Long straight roads ribboned between sculptured hills, with scarcely a glimpse of dwellings—buried in up to ten feet of snow. 'In the interior,' says an old Murray guide, 'it is impossible to travel comfortably before April: the natives live half under ground.' The smoke from holes where chimneys made their passageway was in fact the only sign of many a farm or village. Just before we began to feel marooned in this white world the late sunlight took on a smoky orange hue and we entered the industrial haze of Malatya—a sizeable town with a strong

Armenian trading tradition, noted for its peaches, apricots and grapes. We fought our way through a dense mob of men and youths to a noisy Turistik Hotel with double glazing and stove heating.

At 4.15 am, when a single white thread and a single black could be distinguished in the next day's light, the local muezzin awakened us by loudspeaker: 'Allah-il-Allah.'

This mountain region has only recently been 'discovered' for its flora. In Turkey there are four times as many floral species as in Britain with a distribution of astonishing generosity. To go through by road later in spring is to pass between winding herbaceous borders, always profuse and varied by the altitude. Delphinium, hollyhock, gladiolus, anchusa, ecchium, salvia, sweet pea proliferates at one level; asters, pinks, daphne, pale iris, grape hyacinth, primulas, magenta geranium at another. Higher still blue gentian, viola, scilla, anemone, fritillary and low-growing rhododendron. Often whole meadows are coloured red, yellow, blue, mauve with the seasonal surge of wild flowers. I tried to imagine them as the coach—its engine having been run all night to avoid freeze up—was manoeuvred through the snow from Malatya to Elazig, Tunceli and Erzurum.

We crossed the first, lower levels, dotted with farms, poplars, tiny hamlets and occasional open fields, where whole families were already attacking the snow-streaked soil, without great difficulty. Elazig full of townees in black suits and neb caps, nut-sellers, weighing machines, gimcrack stalls and flashy jewellery shops, seemed an up-country centre for rough country folk. After this the road quickly climbed again to 4,400ft: mountainy men in thick woollen caps or red and yellow turbans cantered by on white ponies, men from the old region of the Dersim Kurds. The gravel road was pitted with pot-holes, the snow banked high. Beyond Tunceli, a small place with some bright modern flats, the cutting through the snow banks had a long frieze of icicles. Between the gleaming cornices, of twice bus height, we were driving through a continuous ice tunnel.

At Pulumur the road reached over 6,000ft, surrounded by mountains up to 10,000ft covered thickly with snow and offering

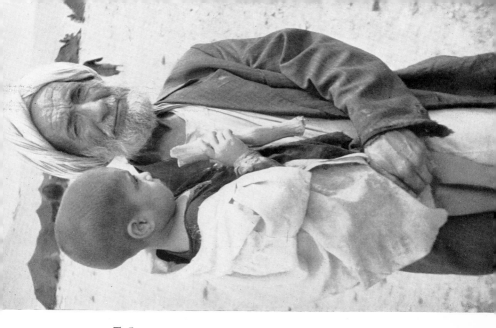

Page 89: *(left)* Nomad matriarch; *(right)* Afghan frontier nomads

Page 90: By the mosque at Kabul; *(right)* on the bund at Kabul

fine ski slopes. Reinforced steel-and-concrete road tunnels were frequent, designed to bolster up scree slopes and divert rock falls and avalanches. We passed many avalanche courses, whose moraine had carved a way down to the floor of the valley : huge balls of snow and blocks of boulder clay marked the abortive start or finish of others. Caterpillar tractors and snow-ploughs were at work clearing blockages. Boulders set in the road warned of recent accidents. Black goats trekked in single file to dumps of fodder across the dazzling virgin slopes.

Before reaching Tunceli we had crossed the Murat river, a tremendous cleft of purplish, green, sulphur-coloured and bituminous rock in which I sighted the first hoopoe. Before Tercan, we crossed the Kara Su (black water) a turbulent, wide and powerful brown river : from the juncture of the two flows the Turkish-named Firat, or in classical terms, the Euphrates. So another boundary was passed, that from Asia Minor, stage on which the historic conflict between East and West has been waged, into the region of the great rivers Euphrates and Tigris, whose southern course encloses the cradle of the human race, and so into Asia proper. The land here had a remote, legendary air. Wooden chalets buried in the snow sent up stove-pipes, like so many periscopes in an undulating white ocean. At 8.30 pm, after over thirteen hours driving, we drew in to the black-ice-covered Dostoyevskyan town of Erzurum.

The droshky drivers in Erzurum wore several layers of over-coats and lined leather helmets with flaps tied under the chin; the breath of their blanketed horses turned to hoar frost in the night air, the yellow side-lamps winked like dying stars. Slab snow was frozen hard and thick on the pavements. Men wore scarves and fur hats over face and ears, women veiled from crown to heel in their chadars were bulked out with layer upon layer of trousers and skirts. We hurried from our rooms at the Lale Palas across the black, glittering square to the welcoming steamy heat of a double-glazed restaurant. Local businessmen were taking their evening relaxation of raki and bowls of pistachio nuts set alight with methylated spirits. We ordered our kebabs and pilafs, our dolma and liver fry. Waiters of old-fashioned formality

F

hovered and bowed, gliding swiftly over the sanded floor among pots of trailing ivy, plastic flowers, shelves of liqueurs and the hissing samovar.

Erzurum, altitude 6,200ft, one-time frontier fortress of the Byzantine Empire, stands some three hundred feet above the great plain of the Kara commanding a magnificent view westwards; to north and south rise lofty mountains; exit to the east is via the 'camel neck' pass. It is said to be famous for beautiful women, good water, superlative tea and cold winters. Frost begins in September, snow may fall until June; winter temperatures drop to 10–25 degrees below zero F. 'Spectacles are indispensable for winter travelling', warn the old guide books. 'They should be kept in place by an elastic cord and no metal be allowed to touch the skin. . . . Few winters pass without some persons perishing in a tipi—a snowstorm accompanied by a strong gale which whirls the fine surface ice-powder into the air and numbs and blinds the traveller.'

Many of Erzurum's flat-roofed houses are covered with two to three feet of earth, for winter protection and in summer a place for sitting out 'on the lawn'. There is much to admire—thirteen minarets in the old town, the unusual twin red-brick minarets of the ruined Seljuk 'madraseh' or college, fluted like Ionic columns and ornamented with a regular pattern of light blue tiles; the old citadel and also the brick-and-tile tower of the barracks in a bright-coloured linked-diamond design. A special flavour goes with Erzurum, the thick fur caps and big flat caps, the white-bearded old men and plumped-out matrons, the rattling droshkies and steaming samovars, the rough-looking streets and bears and wolves in the mountains—a flavour that might seem unchanged since the four years of its Russian occupation following World War I. Readers of *Greenmantle* will recall its winter description as scene of the final showdown, the Cossack charge.

Beyond Agri, in the corner where Georgia, Iran and Turkey come within each other's rifle sights, Mount Ararat rises imperiously to 16,946ft. From a massive base with a spectacular series of rock buttresses, through a waistband of light cloud, its

twin cone-shaped peaks in their perpetual snow held the
apricot light of the afternoon sun. Little Ararat, on the same vast
base (the actual meeting ground of the three powers' territory),
another conical extinct volcano rising to 13,000ft, is dwarfed
in comparison. Called by the Armenians 'Massis', by the Turks
'Egri Dagi' or Painful Mountain, and by the Persian's 'Koh-i-
nuh' or Mountain of Noah, to travellers like ourselves Ararat
indicated both the end and the beginning of a long journey. We
travelled round the treeless lava plain of its base, on which
herds of wild horses wheeled, for half the afternoon, increasingly
aware of the grand scale of this mountain, whose only rivals lie
in the Caucasus, where Mt Elbrus, 18,480ft, is visible from
Ararat's summit some 280 miles away. And in doing so we came
over the last parasangs of Turkey to the frontiers of Persia.

# 4 EAST OF ARARAT

*We consoled ourselves during our stay in Persia by the consideration that we should soon be in Afghanistan.*

Robert Byron

A frontier post is not usually a dull place. Bazargan, our entry point for Iran, was no exception. There were the ochre hills, crystal clear in a blue and white sky, and a rugged horizon, within rifle shot. A Japanese student, small, almost miniaturised, motionless in the dust, waited with a huge 'Cruiser' pack for a lift—to Kathmandu. A couple of three-tier trucks drove up, opened their back-flaps and took aboard about five hundred sheep which had quietly materialised out of the barren hills. Four young men in white overalls, goggles and white vizor-caps came through the barrier nose to tail and shot away in four Mercedes with a great roar of exhaust. 'Delivery drivers,' said Frank. 'Nice job. Thirty-five quid for five days. Then thumb it back to Germany.' . . . A carpet dealer followed, opulent looking as his car-load. We had coffee in the shanty café attached to the post, where a swarthy Persian presided and totted up the total on a well-used abacus. Two Danes appeared, lay flat just outside and proceeded to roast themselves in the sun. Presently the café-owner came out with two heavy wooden clubs, the size and shape of the biggest prize vegetable marrow, and proceeded to do a work-out. He wielded them up and over, behind his shoulders, in circles at his sides, crossing down in front with the ease and controlled breathing of a practised 'Zoor-Khaneh' gymnast. We read the notice again: 'Honourable Ladies and Gentlemen, Passengers, Pilgrims and Tourists, the Customs Office on behalf of the Imperial

Iranian Government and the hospitable Nation of Iran have the honour to welcome you warmly and will greatly appreciate your esteemed views, critics and suggestions.' Then our passports and visas were ready.

The sun was lower as we came into the shadow of the hills. Maku gorge, with its motel and hospital squeezed in below towering brown buttresses of rock, opened out into a fast, nearly level road towards Tabriz. We saw a golden sundown, picking out the purple, copper-green and mahogany ridges beyond the glistening white salt-pans, and the mountains beyond Lake Urmia : we saw wading storks, watched the glow of fires and the lights come on in mud-built villages. Then there was just the road, flung up by the headlights to be swallowed again immediately under the wheels. There was no trouble when we arrived—'TABRIZ : hotels, none, but no difficulty in obtaining shelter and food' (Murray)—although it was close to midnight. The huge glittering necklace of its lights seen from across the plateau indicated the vast area covered by Tabriz's grid-pattern streets. A thirteenth-century mosque—another 'Blue Mosque' veneered in mosaic-tile, and an ancient Ark or citadel, a mountain of small russet bricks, are its chief monuments. It has miles of brick vaulted bazaar and houses a quarter million people. Seen by day the city has a clean, tree-shaded French look about its avenues, a striking, Swiss-built town hall and an agreeable scatter of antique shops. Its museum represents the province of Azerbaijan : its own special artistic tradition lies in fine calligraphy and early bookbinding. To please its founder, his favourite wife, Haroun-el-Rashid frequently chose to reside there. Revisiting Tabriz in summer, after traversing much of the rest of Iran, I admired his choice. A picture that stays in mind is of a Persian home, very late that night, glimpsed from an upper window : the family sat at supper on a glowing red carpet, shoes discarded and dishes of curd, chapatti and rice set out on a cloth. Lamplight kindled their faces, while above and behind the house hills gloomed under a darkened sky.

Road conditions made a detour necessary next day, among the lemon-coloured foothills and through the Takh-rud gorge, with its strongly-built mud villages. The principal houses had courtyards with protective walls; some buildings had wide, plastered porches. Women in bright red or black enveloping chadars could be seen at the well or the stack, but nothing else of man or beast. Each place seemed a fastness, among a wilderness of curving hills. Eventually the gorge debouched into the wide sandy plain before Miyaneh—where we bought dates, nuts and cream cheese with our new rials.

On the way to Zanjan gophers appeared, and buzzards and vultures wheeled overhead. We soared along the blue-black highway between escarpments of pale cream, olive-green, pale-brick banded soils and crags the colour of cornelian or iron-slag deepening to rich purple. Zanjan's green-tiled, diamond-patterned mosque, crowned by a gilded sun and flanked by barley-sugar minarets rose above a maze of cool house alleys in dark gold shadow. Shenar and Ghazvin—several times capital city but now comparatively neglected—came and went in the usual post-Reza Shah style for Persian towns : a roundabout with dry flower beds, dry fountain and stereotyped silver-gilt statue of the present Shah at entry, a long straight street and bazaar mingling mud-brick and fluorescent lighting, then another roundabout with its statue, flower beds and fountain, from which a trail of shacks peters out into the desert. Reza Shah, the Cossack colonel who like his contemporary Ataturk in Turkey, put Iran willy-nilly on the road to modernisation, also put it on the road to standardisation.

After a timeless interval of undeviating, sand-hazed, sun-dazzled speedway, we found ourselves being swallowed, without warning that the desert held such monsters, into the outskirts of a vast, westernised metropolis : a city which, while Tabriz has not quite doubled its population in the last sixty years, has increased ten-fold in half that time.

Until it was adopted as capital by the founder of the Qajar dynasty in 1796, Tehran was quite unimportant. Even fifty years ago to enter it was like entering any other dusty, desert city of uneven mud walls, deep moat, tiled gates and dead animals thrown out for carrion. Its tree-lined streets were full of holes and had open water-channels, diverted for gardens and the basins in courtyards. Dried dung was used for house roofing and fuel. There were swarms of dervishes and beggars: horse-drawn trams; no street lights, no cars, but many camels—and the Shah's elephant. It was best seen by moonlight.

In the last thirty years not only has the population of Tehran increased to over 2,200,000, but its car ownership has multiplied by 10,000! No 'tree-tops showing over the mud walls' now, but everywhere six- or eight-storey buildings and blocks, from twelve to twenty-five storeys, as landmarks to the bewildering complex of squares and avenues. London-red omnibuses, orange taxis, blaring klaxons, Cineramas and dance-clubs, fashion boutiques and antique salons, neon-signs and supermarkets, concrete stadia, consulates and modern factories emphasise a frantic, almost febrile aping of Europe and the USA. Recently a series of reforms in land tenure, suffrage, public investment, profit-sharing and rural welfare, the so-called 'White Revolution' advocated by Shah Mohammed, has given fresh impetus to change. Waiting for evolutionary trends to mould the old Persian feudal structure into a modern 'state economy' appeared far too slow a process. Iran must 'be speeded on the road to membership with the more advanced industrial nations'. Outside observers may feel that older virtues and more colourful traditions are being subordinated to the 'sick culture of huge cinemas, swimming pools, brassières and pants, breasts and sandals and dark glasses', but to many insiders 'the magic is at work in Persia today'.

One feature of old Tehran remains in the same use. A jube, or water channel, runs down each street carrying away the refuse of match boxes, cigarettes ends, vegetable scraps. People come out to wash their radishes or lettuce in it, to empty or rinse tea-pots; children, naturally, add to it; cats and dogs drink from it; in the parks mothers hold out their babies over it; after siesta the young and old wash their faces in it. We were not surprised to notice numbers of blind, one-eyed or wall-eyed beggars, people with protective eye patches or inflammation. It used to be said of Tehran that 'every single act for which water is needed is accomplished openly by the roadside'; it remains a marvel that the Persian does not suffer even more from skin diseases and eye infections.

Another traditional sight attracted us in the City Park—Park-e-Shahr. Behind the phallic monument in aluminium alloy at the main entrance, beyond the geometrical flower beds, the brown grass and the benches with old men and roughs ('thick necks' in Farsi) taking their afternoon sleep, a knot of boys and youths were gathered under some trees from which came the thin sound of music. Edging into the circle we saw a man playing a one-string mandolin and conducting a kind of marionette ballet. Tiny figures including horsemen were made to perform round the rim of a stool or upturned drum by means of strings attached to his fingers on the instrument wires. As he quipped with his audience or sang ballads he kept the puppets moving in time with the tune. The ballet show, called 'Rachs', and the mandolin 'Shypor' seemed as popular with the crowd and the situations as well known as in 'Punch and Judy'.

> The owner of the show talks to the marionettes, asks them questions like the ring-master with the clown in a circus . . . a musician beats a drum and chants appropriate verses. The Shah appears in a carriage drawn by two horses. To amuse his Majesty there are wrestlers, acrobats and dancers: a man receives the bastinado. At the end the devil appears and carries off each marionette in turn except the Shah who slips out. (*Peeps into Persia* by Dorothy de Warzée.)

We had not been in the park more than five minutes before 'youth' approached, in pairs hand in hand. 'What is your name?' 'Where are you going?' 'Where have you come?' 'How old are you?' 'Are you married?' 'You have how many children?' 'What do you work?' 'Do you love Iran?' 'Why do you not photograph it?' They were but repeating class-book phraseology, students of sixteen to twenty all anxious to practise their English, gain a certificate and reach university. There were so few places in Tehran—only one for every eighty applicants. Could we help them to enter college in England, perhaps, and then they could become doctor, engineer, scientist?

Near the Park, in the street of public letter-writers, beggars

whined for alms, displaying their stumps, deformities and para-
lytic tremors. One exposed his stomach which had a hole in it
attached to a rubber bladder, and innumerable workless or work-
shy men offered lottery tickets, matches, combs, nuts, used stamps,
old coins. Street markets were in full swing, crammed with shiny
materials, silks, ribbons, glass, plastic, their kerosene lamps blaz-
ing away in daylight on raucous salesmen. The New Year ('No
Ruz' 22 March) spirit was abroad: lights everywhere, bursts of
fireworks or thrown 'crackers', children parading with henna'd
beards, masks, drums and pipes, a few 'mummers' in fools caps,
red pierrot suits, banging their tambourines and blowing shrill
whistles. At a money-changers' we were given presents of 'fool's
gold' tokens in addition to the rial rate. At a popular supper
place just off Eslambul, a sitar band came round and Indo-
Iranian music surged as we ate our appetisers of radish and
onion, before a great dish of chicken, rice, herbs and beans, and
arak or Shiraz wine.

At our modest hotel in Lalezar—an old street leading to the
Bazaar—noise knew no bounds. The manager's office window
opened over a ground-floor drinking hall, where the belly-dancers
who performed twice nightly were real Scheherezades, not the
ballet-school beginners of Istanbul: the tumblers and acrobats
performed somersaults to land on each others' upraised feet, back-
wards and blindfold. When the belly-dance rhythms had begun
to subside under the rooms on one side of the corridor, under
the windows of those on the other were the crowds coming riot-
ously home until 3 am from club, dance-hall or cinema which
occur every few yards through the length of Lalezar, sleazier and
more stereophonic the nearer they approach the bazaar.

'A graceless capital in a setting of grandeur', one cynic said.
No one seems completely taken in by Tehran; not even the
Iranians.

It lacks beauty, though it is not without charm. The effect is
rather as if it had sprung up overnight out of the earth with its
tentacles spreading across what, only yesterday, was still part of
the desert. It is a city without a memory.

The climate is peculiar : some say spring is best, others summer, and call spring overpraised. The feature that explains all this caginess and makes possible Tehran's existence in an otherwise waterless desert, is the massive snow-white backdrop towering at the end of every avenue, of the Elburz mountains and the giant volcanic peak beyond, Damavand, 18,963ft, glittering against a gentian sky. The effect is startling, magnificent, although a gusty, dusty wind blows and the gentian turns to grey one is still conscious of this mountain presence : there is a kind of electricity in the air. Some find it irritating—tempers in Tehran quickly become short—others stimulating. At any rate this is 'the most prominent object about Tehran and the one remembrance of which the traveller longest retains' (Murray).

A modern panorama of the city shows its Labour Bank, Hypotheque Bank, Police fortress and Foreign Ministry buildings viewed from Sepah Square with the Elburz behind. Much more attractive is the Royal Palace called, from its main court, the Gulistan or Garden of Roses. Its pine- and plane-shaded grounds enclose an air of dignity and quiet; its state rooms and their cabinets contain a fascinating mixture of the priceless and the monstrous. The walls of the grounds are set with tiles decorated with peacocks, roses, hoopoes, huntsmen and abstract, Paisley pattern designs. The palace exterior resembles white lace and sugar icing : the entrance hall is a multi-faceted, mirror-mosaic reflecting light from three great Venetian crystal chandeliers. Red-carpeted marble stairs, which we ascended behind the 'ferrashes' or ushers, led to a spacious suite, tile-friezed and embellished with delicate, flowered plasterwork. Its chandeliers, touched with red and blue and its exquisite figured carpets in Assyrian style provided the background to the incredible hoard. Sèvres porcelain, Chinese ginger jars, mother-of-pearl tables, vases given by the Czar Nicholas, an enormous clock from Queen Victoria, jewel-encrusted plates, Victorian Gothic chairs with antlers for arms and legs, ornaments in green marcasite, chairs in mustard yellow plush, great services of French and English china, chess tables and of course, in one of the state rooms, the gilded thrones brought back from Delhi in 1739 by Nader Shah.

His attack through to India was Persia's reply to a devastating Afghan invasion that cost a million lives and sounded the death knell of the Mughul Empire. The copy of the famous Peacock Throne of the Great Mogul is really a huge litter; both thrones are heavily encrusted with emeralds. In times of financial crisis, many of the orginal gems have been replaced by brilliants. The surviving portion of the genuine Peacock Throne, valued at £12,000,000 in the eighteenth century, and the crown jewels which include an encrusted globe reputedly worth a million sterling in 1900, are kept in the Bank Markasi. Along the corridors and in the ante-chambers of the palace hang a collection of pictures ranging from portraits of friendly monarchs in all varieties of ceremonial garb and moustached panoply to the sun-set-in-the-Alps and Moonlight-in-Venice type of oils.

On the morning we left Tehran I took a stroll about 6 am. Trees cast their lacy pale-shadowed patterns on smooth, swept pavements. From crossings free of traffic one glimpsed long mud-brick alleys of obscure forgotten houses : some older shop fronts had fascia patterns in mosaic tile. Cats quietly explored the backyards of restaurants and rear exits of cinemas; a match-seller was meticulously arranging his corner stall; a fruit-seller had brought out his baskets and begun to set his plums and cherries in nests of vine leaves. The white-moustached and bearded proprietor of a café came to the door in sabots for his bottle of milk. A 'French spoken' creamery was just opening and a 'German spoken' shop selling crisp bread. The clutter of pavement displays—old coins, broken ceramics, medals, magazines, hopelessly hopeful 'art' had not yet accrued. Nobody stood to inveigle customers into the expensive emporia of Avenue Ferdowski. There was a delicacy, a freshness, an unhurried air that might have been Parisian. If one is to be a regular boulevardier of Tehran this is the time to choose—when all the thrusters of the business world and hurtling taxi men are still in their 'takht-e-khab' or thrones of sleep.

We drove south, through the dusty proletarian purlieus beyond the bazaar and railway station, past the tyre and edible oil factories, cement plants and truck assembly yards, into an outskirt area of irrigated fields, almond orchards and vineyards.

Desert air felt all the sweeter after urban fumes, glitter, rush and temptations to indulgence. Cities like Tehran, Istanbul, Beirut have a demoralising effect on the spirit of the long distance traveller. But once in the open desert among the pale, mirage-like tints of sandy-grey and dusty pink or the sandy-green patches of sparse vegetation, under the sandy-blue of a dusty sky, where all perspective is lost in space, a sense of timelessness takes over. The immediate past quickly fades into the endless present : remote history and the living moment seem the same. A 'schimal' was blowing, a strong south-westerly wind setting up willy-willies of dust and for long stretches the coach was encapsulated in a world within a world among clouds of sand, all other modes of existence lost or vanished.

At Saveh, the usual pattern of township with its two round-abouts, statues and straggling bazaar, we explored the back lanes during 'tea-stop'. They led between high mud walls, by blind corners and right-angled turns to an interior square—the real town of the families and household chores. Women enveloped in dark spotted chadars, an end caught in their teeth to conceal the face gave us salaams; girls carried waterpots on their heads, dusty children grinned and japed and ran away. Small openings in the walls led to their own private world of courtyard and carpet, charcoal and cooking pot. The life of such towns is not that seen by the passer-by on the road : the villages, clusters of beehive shaped mud dwellings surrounded by a stout mud-brick palisade, lie well out in the desert, indifferent to modern traffic.

At Delijan, a village of cupolas, the track leads on towards mountains the hue of wine, topped by silvery peaks. Here, in the wastes of this sun-coloured land is the country of the peasants and nomads, the older Iran. Real wealth still lies in the land : even in Tehran and the other twelve main cities, only about five per cent of the people are industrial workers. Water is a problem, but the line of mounds one sees strung out into the desert indicates occasional conduits, 'Kanaats', underground.

We glided on towards Meimeh, over a landscape of wide, level plain ringed on the far horizon by conical peaks, scalloped escarpments, sharp-toothed ridges and distant gleaming moun-

tains. Occasional camel trains plodded along in the sand beside
the tarmac or donkeys burdened with huge string bags of
wool. There were glimpses of mud-walled estates with many-
domed storehouses, of fortified settlements in the foothills, sometimes areas of dry, sparse grass and flocks guarded by a shepherd
bundled up in stiff felt cape. Mazes of ochre foothills and slopes
of pure copper green led up to crags as plum red as those in
Glen Torridon. Wherever there was a water channel there were
wagtails tittuping; once there was an eagle, squatting tamely on
the road edge not twenty yards away, brown, broad-winged,
huge-beaked. Nearby a roadside direction read : GOLD MINES.
(The alternative route from Tabriz comes in over this colourful
terrain, via Kermanshah, Hamadan—the old capital of Media
'Ecabatana' and Iran's oldest extant city—and the pleasant,
French-looking Arak, direct to Isfahan, a route useful for linking
up with Baghdad.)

At Murchen-Khort the old fortified town lies only just off the
road. Each side wall is several hundred yards long, with high
rounded corner towers. There was a small entrance gate facing
the open desert. Two or three of us went through and found ourselves in an enclosed roadway round the inner town. This also
had a gate—but before we could pass through a young man in air
force blue confronted us. Politely he asked the usual questions,
politely but firmly indicated that the inner town, of perhaps
1,000 inhabitants, was not for visitors. He was one of the new
Education Corps, a graduate conscript doing army duty not in
barracks, but in outlying rural areas in the battle against ignor-
ance, illiteracy and isolation under the 'White Revolution',
scheme.

The roadside café had an Arabian Nights atmosphere. Fine
rugs and carpets lined the walls, carpets covered the benches and
on the raised dais, which occupied almost all the floor space of
an inner room, one large carpet of beautiful texture and design
served as bed for travellers beleaguered for the night.

As day faded the lion-coloured hills turned to amethyst and
old rose : odd truncated cones of mountain peaks were theatrically etched against the blue-green sky. The mud-walled wells,

honeycombs of store houses and sheds, the square-walled villages with plant-pot shaped towers became one with the desert. On the southern horizon, where the sky was lavender-edged, a great crescent of denticulated mountain shapes, the Kuh-i-Sufi, 'shaped like Punch's hump', and other ranges appeared backed by jagged snow peaks. Their distance on this wide unvarying plain was deceptive, but 'mountains of singular serrated outline', they signalled the not-so-distant presence of Isfahan.

A few cities strike straight to eye, heart and mind, however brief the traveller's stay. Isfahan is one. Its oasis setting at 5,300ft up in a seventy mile long, twenty mile wide plain, backed by those extraordinary mountains, is incomparable. Its lovely, airy, silver-and-green foliaged, almost insubstantial main thorough-fare and many-bridged river walks, under a sky of liquid violet-blue after the seemingly endless arid, stony desert, are like manna. Its Maidan-i-Shah, one of the largest squares in the world, its mosques, palaces, colleges and unrivalled Imperial Bazaar take the mind back to the Safavid dynasty, before the Afghan invasion, when this was Shah Abbas's capital of Persia. Its merchants and their merchandise are rich and strange as ever, their reputation unique : 'the merchant of Isfahan will put his cheese in a bottle and rub his bread on the outside to give it a flavour.' Isfahan, say Iranians is half the world.

Almost opposite the pleasant hotel, in whose large courtyard rooms we laid our bedrolls, rose the twin, slender minarets of the mosque Soltani Madraseh, looking out across the carriageways, the cycle-paths, the water-channels, flower-beds and translucent green poplar trees of Chahar Bagh—where even the police walk hand-in-hand. This mosque has apparently suffered little since it was built under the Safavids three centuries ago. It is a theological school with a great complex of cubicles and prayer halls, arches and niches, including an exquisite 'mihrab' facing Mecca, and no fewer than 134 rooms. Its great doors are covered with silver plate; its minarets and arches, its lintels and honey-combed recesses are clad in magnificent porcelain tiles or panels of enamelled arabesques, characterised by their geometrical design. The radiance, the colour, the sheer scale and architectural complexity dazzle and bemuse. From the prayer gallery of a minaret—reached by climbing a narrow spiral in absolute darkness—one confronts at only a few yards' distance the huge dome of the mosque: a fabulous egg of turquoise tile, patterned with yellow, green and blue flowers and topped by a gilded crescent and star, glittering in the sun. It seems close enough to touch. And there spread out below is the whole oasis of enamelled minarets, blue cupolas, enclosed gardens, winding river and straight silvery trees, the broad avenues and close, shady alleys extending to the shimmering verge of the desert, a lake of greenness under a sky of boundless blue.

Chahar Bagh, favourite promenading street linked by the Siosepol or Allahverdi bridge to a similar avenue south of the river and the royal vista, is altogether two and a half miles long. The bridge, built by Allahverdi Khan, a general of Shah Abbas, claims to be the finest in the world. It is certainly one of the most remarkable. Nearly a quarter of a mile in length it has thirty-three arches and three promenades, a vaulted passage below, a roadway with side galleries above and an open footpath on top. Rows of large cut-waters project out into the river and the whole structure resembles a series of cloisters of honey-coloured brick and stone. On the north side are car showrooms and cinemas—one was showing *Far from the Madding Crowd* with sub-titles in Farsi—then, until the junction with Sepah Avenue half-way down, there are stores, restaurants, ornamental arches and scores of antique shops. So rich is the display of miniatures, filigree silver, gold, enamels, cut and uncut stones, rugs, embroidery and ceramics, lapis lazuli seals, that Sotheby's run collectors' trips to Isfahan.

Beside Sepah Avenue are the grounds of the Royal Palace, where the statehood of Shah Abbas, a contemporary of Charles I, is reflected in an entrance Pavilion of Forty Columns—twenty real, twenty mirrored in the long pool. Chihil Sutun is a lyrical building in a lyrical setting. From the outside it has a Chinese air, seen across wide green lawns, flower-beds and still water. Within it is all mirror-facet inlay and elaborate cellular ceilings. Beyond was the throneroom and behind it again the great hall, whose murals are now being restored to their original colours. The scenes—of hunting and battle, including Nader Shah's attack on the Indians, and of royal hospitality to Mughul rulers—are as rich in texture as the Canterbury Tales : the banquets show the same fruit, wine vessels, Persian rugs, dress and facial styles as one sees in the roadside picnics of Isfahanis today. Only the jewels and the dancing girls are extra.

In the Maidan itself, Ali Qapu pavilion ('Highest Gate' or 'Sublime Porte') has an audience room above the doorway from which the Shah could watch tournaments in the great square— formerly sanded as a polo ground. The threshold which dates from Tamerlane's time (his sweeping conquests reached Persia in the 1380s), is of green porphyry and was a sacred place of refuge, never crossed on horseback even by Shah Abbas himself. The interior, three storeys high, is a labyrinth of corridors, halls and stairways, with delicate murals of birds, flowers and animals etched on the plaster, still being uncovered from beneath eight overlaid layers by Italian workmen. One room above all deserves notice, on the topmost storey. It has a double structure, the under layer being fretted with openings in the shapes of musical in-struments and the whole forming a sounding box, so that music performed there could be transmitted to the royal audience on the floor below. Its intricate honeycomb pattern provided the 'Hi-Fi' of the age.

Around the Maidan, imperial centre of Shah Abbas, now bright with fountains, flowers and trees in new leaf, cluster the rest of Isfahan's craftware and antique shops in two tiers of blind, white-washed arcades. Enamel and filigree silver, porcelain, brocade and illuminated manuscripts are crammed into the win-dows; copper and tinware, great bowls, trays, kettles, vases, lamp-stands, plaques with Beardsleyesque engraving, overflow on to the pavement under the trees and awnings. Outside one shop a boy of seven or eight sits on the ground with a shining tray on sup-ports. He holds a four inch nail and with blows of a hammer drives it to mark out the peacock pattern in indented points. The sun blazes on the metal, his head comes close to his hand, already his eyes are red and sore : the cost of handwork at cheap price

Page 107: Taj Mahal, Agra

Page 108: (left) Temple entrance, Amber, Rajasthan; (right) a pilgrim at the Golden Temple, Amritsar

is blindness. Down a neighbouring alley, a woman and her daughter of six or seven sit on the mud floor of a room before two looms, 6ft by 12ft. The looms are strung vertically with fibres of tough silk into which the workers weave and knot coloured wools at great speed. Loose ends are cut off roughly with a knife and when a row is finished it is pushed down with a metal comb to blend with the rest and trimmed with scissors. The carpet pattern is shown on a graph-lined card: when it is complete, in two years, it will be worth £300. The woman gets 5 rials per 12ft knotted row, sitting there all day and working at great speed with fingers covered by a hard, thick skin (180r=£1).

Opposite Ali Qapu stands the Sheikh Lutfullah or Ladies' Mosque, its dome reflected in the Maidan's central pool. The Imperial Mosque, Masjid-i-Shah, is at the further end facing the Imperial Bazaar, so that the whole of this formal space is occupied by a romantic diversity of buildings. The beautiful domes of these two Safavid mosques, the smaller a flowered saucer dome covered in creamy tiles patterned with blue and ochre on which a bold-branching rose-tree is inlaid in black and white, the larger imperial dome all greens and blues, seem iridescent bubbles about to rise from earth altogether, floating into and fusing with the luminous sky as the sun strikes them with a broken highlight. The misty blue façade of Lutfullah and its hanging cornices, the doorway and mihrab are especially lovely: within, all symptoms of construction disappear in a mirage of shallow curved surfaces swimming above the ring of sixteen windows. The interior of the dome is decorated with unglazed tiles, a background for floral designs in turquoise, wine, dark blue and black, which make a depth of striking colour as the highlights are again broken by the play of glazed and unglazed surfaces. Its walls, bordered by broad white inscriptions on dark blue, are inlaid with twisting arabesques or baroque squares on deep ochre stucco. To Iranians this is the favourite building in all Isfahan; to Europeans it is a revelation of the splendours to be achieved with abstract patterns.

Shah Mosque was built late in the Shah's reign, hurried to completion—but not until after his death—by the use of coarse floral tile-work instead of mosaic to cover the walls. Its very size

G

conveys the feeling of a mausoleum. The monumental doorway is immense, the basement being paved with marble. The floor of the part used by worshippers is covered in turquoise tiles. The proportions are majestic. There is a riot of colour everywhere, but the fountains are empty. Among the great echoing prayer halls and pointed ivans one could easily miss an exceptionally fine mosaic panel, a veritable Garden of Eden, with peacocks, animals, flowers, trees and birds of paradise.

One of the best times for visiting the Imperial Bazaar is late afternoon. After a cooling glass of 'masht'—iced sour milk—we sauntered between the deep shadows and bright shafts of sunlight from the blue ceiling holes of the vaulted aisles, stopping to gaze at almost every stall. Manufactures of all kinds are displayed—fabrics from velvet to calico, spices and soaps, guns and sword-blades, glassware and gold, ropes and leather-work, sweetmeats and string. Crafts of all kinds are carried on in the cavernous workshops from dyeing to wood-turning, saddlery to tinsmithing. There are dozens of bric-à-brac stalls—some with very curious examples of Persian painting focused on the female pudenda—set among exquisitely finished papiermâché pencil cases decorated with Victorian costume scenes. In a semi-underground retreat a camel, blindfold, walks round and round harnessed to a heavy beam which controls a roller crushing seeds into a tub for dye: it might be one of the punishments in a medieval dungeon. In another Faginesque den the dyeing is in progress: skeins of wool in metal baskets are lowered into steaming cauldrons of liquid and after the dye has taken, raised to the roof for the wool to dry glowing brilliantly in the sun. Horses decorated with fringes of beads pull carts up and down the alleys. At a junction a grey-bearded man sells iced green figs in sweet syrup from a three hundred year old Persian bowl. Round a corner steps lead down to the 'hummum', its entrance bright with blue mosaic tiles showing figures bathing. The main entrance has a huge, old clay-coloured arch decorated with remains of mosaics (called Nakkara Khaneh). Beside it a grizzled beggar, almost black with exposure, strips himself naked to pick the fleas out of his tattered sheepskin coat. In and out, hissing a warning to pedestrians,

errand boys on bicycles scurry among the crowds with the agility
of acrobats.

At six again on our last morning I slipped out of the hotel into
Chahar Bagh. Only sweepers and labourers going to work on
silent bicycles stirred the fresh desert air, sparkling with light and
with the light green leaves of white-stemmed poplars. Soltani
Madraseh's dome looked as insubstantial as a thrush's eggshell.
I turned down a narrow way, where a clear stream ran beside
the cycle path and a crumbling wall bulged out dangerously
at corners. In the little streets leading down to the river there were
green-shuttered houses and green doors with hand-shaped brass
knockers. Occasionally a side door gave glimpses of a sunken pool
and flower garden. Birds sang in cages hung from the mud-brick
walls. 'Kif' in 'Loti'-land again . . .

Beyond the suburbs, Julfa, the Christian quarter, and the airport, we came to wide 'sage-brush' desert. The road traverses
wild undulating country, region of the Bakhtiari, Qashquai and
other nomads, where the 'Tchador-neshin' (those who live in
tents) move their herds from pasture to pasture. As it crosses the
high central plateau, reaching 7,500ft, the lonely ribbon of tarmac might equally be in Utah as in Fars. There are gorges to
cross—including a pass, 'Queh-Kush', feared even by gipsies for
its icy, killing wind—tilted red-ochre, grey or greenish strata, cut-
off flat-topped volcanoes and distant snow-veined mountains.
The tents, black felt  shaggily roofed with straw, hug sheltered
depressions, square forts crown the heights. The Qashquai headgear is seen, a felt cap with ear pieces, and Bakhtian trousers,
flapping wide and black. Women in ankle-length frilled dresses
of pink, strawberry, bright green, orange with gold spangles and
bright headscarves, flounce proudly along. A pinkish-purple
lavender grows among the sandy screes and there are endless
stones.

We cross the plateau from the walled village of Abadeh
(famous for its shoes) to Deh-Bid and Abbas-Abad; then there is
a gradual descent. Stagnant pools and a few lime-green trees give
Persians on their way to Persepolis and Shiraz a place to spread
picnic rugs by water—or in the dark overhang of roadside cliffs,

in this 'home province' of Persia. Sixty kilometres or so short of
Shiraz we find the place to camp and stumbling across the sand
to the shelter of a patch of scrub, set up tents and stoves as
Alexander the Great's soldiers must have done, almost on the
threshold of Persepolis.

At dawn there is skim-ice on the water-bucket, frosty rime on
the tent flaps and a champagne sparkle in the desert, whose midday air 'too fine to describe, tells of perfect loneliness, dried grass
and the sun on burning flint' (T. E. Lawrence). A woman and
dog are already watchful from the scatter of roadside shanties.
Presently she comes across with small glasses of tea on a battered
brass tray; we break some hard chapatti, add a handful of dates
and that is breakfast.

Persians, whose assertive pride tends to focus on their
westernisation, are justifiably proud of their ancient monuments,
claiming their civilisation as the oldest in the world—'six thousand
years of uninterrupted culture'—and the first world conquest that
of Cyrus. The lowlands of Persia, between the Karun and the
Tigris, have the earliest known settled-city sites: some bronzes
found in Luristan date from 4000 BC; Kashan, Saveh, Qom have
yielded almost as ancient pottery. Cyrus the Persian took Babylon
from the Assyrians and within a generation Darius the Great extended the first Aryan empire from the Indus to the Danube,
from the Aral Sea to the Blue Nile. (He was brought to a halt
only by the Greeks at Marathon.) Persepolis or 'Takht-e-Jamsid',
the throne of the mythical king, is a monument of pride. Begun
by Darius about 518 BC and continued by his son Xerxes and his
grandson, it spells out the imperial concept, the achievements and
power of the Achaemenids. It is the dynastic shrine of 'the great
King, King of Kings, King of lands peopled by many races,
King of this great wide earth, son of Hystaspes, the Achaemenian,
a Persian, son of a Persian and Aryan of Aryan descent', as
Darius's tomb inscription declares in three languages.

The whole of Persepolis, primarily a platform almost 1,500ft
long and nearly 1,000ft wide, rising between 20 and 50ft above
the plain, partly hewn from the solid rock, has a celebrational
character. Its most striking dynastic feature is the bas-relief which

covers the eastern supporting walls of the double staircase leading up to the Apadana, or Audience Hall, and shows the scale of the homage paid to Darius. In the centre are four Achaemenid guards and the lion of Iran devouring the Assyrian bull; to the right a procession of subject peoples bringing their ' No-Ruz' tribute of livestock, grain, silk and wine to the king; to the left a royal guard of Medes and Persians, infantry, archers, cavalry, charioteers, the Persians being distinguished by the similarity of their caps to those worn today. The subject procession, in three series of twenty-two tableaux divided by the cypress of Shiraz, includes among its twenty-eight races: Africans, Arabs, Greeks, Indians, Scythians, Assyrians, and people from Balkh, Bokhara and Korasan in characteristic costume and with associated animals: giraffes, camels, sheep, zebras and dromedaries. The total impression is of supreme confidence, exuberance and discipline. In the brilliant sunshine of this early morning the forceful carvings seemed to hold the life of only yesterday.

One looks again at the Persian officers, with their hair standing out in tight curls, beards in fine orderly waves, moustaches half concealing curled lips, high cheekbones, wide nostrils, almond eyes: with a slight trim they are the inhabitants of modern Iran.

The scale of Persepolis is grandiose. Darius's great Audience Hall could hold ten thousand people; only thirteen of its original thirty-six fluted columns still stand. They are of white marble weathered to cream or brown, with a pinkish glow, but not that sense of absorbed sunshine which is the beauty of the Parthenon. On the great rock platform there were also Darius's Palace or Banquet Hall, Palaces of Xerxes and Artaxerxes, and extending from the southern balcony a hanging garden in Babylonian style, which looked over the wide, mountain-ringed plain. The Treasury, represented by the remains of two great halls and staterooms, occupies almost a quarter of the site. Still larger in scale is the Hall of a hundred columns or Throne Hall, where the king is shown seated while the twenty-eight nations of his empire support his throne. It was this hall that suffered most when Alexander captured and fired Persepolis in 330 BC. But although the brick palaces have crumbled, the woodwork of beams and ceilings perished, the pillars lost their capitals and been broken into fragments, the magnitude and energy of what remains are imperial eloquence itself.

On the eastern cliff-side, above the palaces, there are the tombs of two of the last Achaemenid kings. The façade represents a palace in bas-relief and there is a great frieze showing the king, bow in hand, worshipping at the fire altar and symbol of the sun. The ground here is covered with wild stocks, delicate mauve in colour and strongly scented. This and the Gatehouse of All Nations, carved with huge, human-headed winged bulls, by which we left the ruined capital, descending the grand stairway of shallow steps built for mounted horsemen, spoke again of the soaring pride and inevitable course of all empires:

> They say the Lion and the Lizard keep
> The courts where Jamshyd gloried and drank deep;
> And Bahram, that great Hunter—the Wild Ass
> Stamps o'er his head, and he lies fast asleep.
> (Rubaiyat of Omar Khayyám)

The saltpan desert Dasht-e-Kavir comes nearest to the road on approaching Ali-Abad, north of Qom (second most holy, golden-domed city of Iran, at times virtually closed to non-Mohammedans). The great pans lie like lakes of milk against the pale colours of the mountains and the paler sky as unreal as if seen through butter muslin. There are sharp indentures of shadow where water-scored channels have carved through the surface, and a few clusters of desert flowers, chiefly the globe thistle, a lovely blue ball emerging from its rosette of silvery-grey foliage. We consult maps and work out that from Ali-Abad a roadless, if not trackless desert extends eastwards for seven hundred kilometres before meeting the route to Meshed. In the south the Great Salt merges with the Great Sand Desert Dasht-e-Lut extending almost to the latitude of Shiraz and the Persian Gulf. It is possible to cross it from corner to corner, 'an arduous and testing journey': some Land-Rover parties do. Bob and the MCW prefer the Caspian route for Meshed.

The barrier of the Elburz, between Tehran and the Caspian, is negotiated by one of the most dramatic highways in Iran. There is a long climb to the pass, by the spa of Abali, by a new winter sports centre, and near to the circuitous route to the Valley of the Assassins, inaccessible for six months of the year. It comes almost to the base of Mount Damavand and is varied with fearsome gorges, fantastically contorted rock strata, long curves of rock tunnels, glissades of water slides, great spreads of avalanche débris and remote encampments of nomads. The variety of Persian landscape, from salt-pan desert to rock gorge and precipice, is further emphasised in the descent, on the Caspian side, from tundra type vegetation, through lush green forests—beach, oak, acacia, tamarisk and bracken—to a coastal plain of rice paddies, cotton and tobacco fields.

From such towns as Amol and Sari, with their quiet, shady mud-walled lanes, flower-and-bird painted plasterwork, sunny courtyards and domed brick hummums in dusty squares and their women in Caucasian dress, one takes a local bus and within half an hour can enjoy the limitless expanse of Riviera-like beaches. There are no seagulls, no starfish, no limpets, no crabs; just sand-pipers, dunes, purple sea-thistle and the gently rolling Caspian with its floor of warm sand. If it is hot, women may come and bathe in their cotton trousers and long-sleeved blouses, then retire to the protection of bamboo screens.

The main road offers only a distant glimpse of sea across level flats, dotted with grazing mares under a soft blue haze of sky, as far as Gorgan and the fringe of Turkoman country, where black fleece hats, slit eyes and small horses fancifully recall portraits of Tamerlane, the Turkoman from Samarkand. In Gorgan market square a temple was hung with black banners and crowned with a diadem of lights : black streamers and pennants fluttered from houses and shops and the men wore black turbans in seasonal mourning for Fatima the chaste, whose shrine is at Qom.

Beyond Shah-Pasand the road abruptly ceases to be 'trunk' quality. For the next day and a half it was to be unmetalled, gravelly dust road, the 'new military road' of the thirties. 'Usable in most places, subsidiary roads may give trouble to old cars

in most places, subsidiary roads may give trouble to old cars
during floods and in winter,' remarks the Irani Guide. 'The road
via the northern highway (from Tehran to Meshed) is not first
class, but what the tourist can see compensates for the discomforts
of this journey.' So speed was reduced but the chassis juddered
violently over concealed potholes and within half a mile had shed
exhaust pipe, radiator grid, fore and aft 'crash bars', lamps and
a section of side panel. With the engine-plate held by one rivet
we pressed on through the dust and in gathering darkness, unable
to appreciate the wild game reserves and the beauties of the gorge
towards Dasht. The dim lights of Bodjnoord at last appeared. We
stayed in a typical Persian old-style caravanserai; a quadrangle
with rooms for cooking, eating and communal sleeping just within the arched entrance, and beyond rows of small rooms, almost
cells, round the other sides, a central well and stabling.

The bump-grind highway led next day through picturesque
reaches of Scottish-lakes scenery to Shirvan and Ghoochan.
There were beech and alder copses, glades starred with buck-
thorn blossom, scillas and yellow tigerlilies (Lilium Ponticum),
bright streams and turfy clearings. At times gazelles glided swiftly
across our view. The villages had round mud houses, large green
mounds (flood sites perhaps for dwellings) and towers of refuge
for defence, formerly, against Turkoman marauders.

In Ghoochan we watched the ceremonial departure of a
mullah to the bus for Mecca. He walked in slow state down the
middle of the road in orange-gold turban and blue frockcoat,
receiving embraces and kisses on his bearded cheeks and mittened
hands from men in long 'poshtins' or jackets bound at the waist
by coloured cummerbunds. Women wore deep blue and white
spotted chadars or green, blue, red, orange trousers tight at the
ankle : many had large ear-rings and necklaces of coins. A new
note in men's headgear was struck by a hard, round brimless hat;
some older women had dyed their shoulder-length hair red and
tattooed their mouths and chins dark blue. Youths had one palm
dyed ochre; and donkeys had ochre hand-marks on their backs.
There were many sightless eyes and alopecia-patched heads. At
the street corner a Mongolian-featured old man squatted on his

heels smoking a long, wooden opium* pipe. Droshkies tinkled past upholstered with eiderdown or patchwork quilting in pink and blue. Rough dogs prowled the stalls; snow was piled in the sheltered courtyard of the mosque. The USSR boundary was only thirty or forty miles away.

The barriers of Meshed are religious. This star-shaped city has an average of a thousand pilgrims every day of the year and a floating population of 25,000 in addition to its own 200,000 inhabitants. Its inner circle of mausoleum, mosque, madraseh surrounded by the booths and labyrinthine lanes of a Moslem market, one can perambulate only on the outside. If the 'mashdi' or townspeople do not hiss their warning to any stranger who wanders beyond the splendid golden gate, endowed by Nader Shah, to the sanctuary precinct or who tries to explore the jewellery stalls within the market enclosures, guards or janitors with silver mace soon usher him away. The tomb of the martyr, Ali-Reza, the eighth Shi'ite Imam, buried next to the Caliph Haroun el-Rashid, is sacred; its gold helm-shaped dome and gold minarets, the huge sea-blue bulbous dome, inscribed in bold black Kufic, and the enormous minarets of the mosque that was built by Gohar Shad, wife of Shah Rukh, son of Timur, are only for the faithful—unless one is accommodated with a suitable robe and smuggled in by a mashdi. So the 'finest surviving expression of the Timurids' is invisible for non-Moslems. Only at Herat where some ruined minarets of Gohar Shad's other mosque survive, can one get an idea of 'marble panels carved with a baroque Kufic, yellow, white, olive-green and rusty red mingling with blues in a maze of flowers, arabesques and texts as fine as the pattern on a tea-cup'. But even less holy places in Persia were only furtively opened to non-believers for the first time in 1931. But men, and women, if totally veiled, may enter the museum of the shrine. We did. It contains one of the world's finest carpet collections, illuminated Korans, oriental blue and white porcelain and celadon ware, pearl and silver thread tapestries, ceremonial armour and inlaid thrones. The latter were devoutly kissed by the crowd, a dense throng kept moving by the attendants.

* In Tehran some 600lbs of opium are consumed—usually in secret—per day.

Four radiating tree-lined avenues, with their modern buildings
and shops, converge on the grand circus which insulates the
sacred centre. The people here make Meshed's fascination. The
whole street that rings the precinct is packed with stalls and
shops, but the passers-by leave one barely chance to notice them.
They are like the company of Chaucer's pilgrims easternised:
chanting blind beggars in pairs, bread sellers with huge brass
scales, letter-writers squatting on the pavement, acrobats with
stilts, men with huge swollen scrota, hip-deformed girls, ascetic
mullahs in grey surtouts, snowy turbans and brown kaftans, street
barbers, toad-faced women, women looking like lepers or 'calico
beehives with a window at the top' in their enveloping white
burquas with netted eye-holes, jackanapes youth as everywhere.
There are Turkomans, people of Afghanistan and Kurdistan,
Arabs, Pakistanis, central Asians: tall, humorous men smoking
hookahs, odd men in corners reading the Koran, sellers of
'prayer stones'—small inscribed bricks of clay from Medina or
from Qom, to which the kneeling faithful bow their foreheads—
sellers of rings set with moonstone, agate and turquoise, men
cutting hens' throats and bleeding them into the gutter, Kurdish
herdsmen with tasselled black scarves wound round their heads
driving sheep along the pavement, men carrying green parrots in
cages or balancing trays of yellow pansy plants on their heads.
And round this human circus prance horses with arches of bells
above their heads, pulling brightly striped and fringed cabs carrying veiled women. In their direction or near the mosque cameras
must *not* be pointed.

A call at the Afghan Embassy, a further dose of anti-cholera
pills, purchase of some boiled eggs, bread, gherkins, sausage and
chocolate, and we were off by the dusty road across river beds
and three-hundred-year-old bridges to Fariman and Torbat Jam.
Yellow dust infiltrated everywhere; willy-willies stalked the
rolling plain; the hills were dark blue streaked with white under
the high cumulus of a Paul Henry landscape. Old forts and
straggling mud villages clung to the road; in some of the fields
men dug with chain-spades or harrowed with bullocks dragging
a log: there were cone-shaped storage structures with projecting

beams to support hay. The twisted wreck of a Volkswagen near the frontier advertised the occupational risk of the hash-smuggler's career, as Frank, driver for the day, pointed out.

At the customs post a clerk in blue pyjamas and white shirt entertained our wait with expert variations of key and rhythm on a two-string guitar. A last glass of hot sweet tea, sitting cross-legged in a small shop of Torbat Jam's tree-lined single street, with the scent of dust and oleanders, the grins of children seeking foreign stamps and hoping for spare rials, and a sudden incursion of large-winged beetles was our farewell to a country as big as the whole of France, Spain, Italy and Great Britain put together.

First stop in Afghanistan was at a nomad encampment. A cluster of black, bat-like tents hugged the low ridge below the skyline : a herdsman leaned on his staff between his flock and the road. We were moving slowly; he beckoned and we stopped. Could we take an old man into town? seemed to be the message of his gesture and signs. In return, then, could we visit the tents?

We crossed the sandy scrub, dotted with yellow starwort and the sinister, fetid dragon arum with thick, shiny black spadix and livid chocolate-purple 'flower', up to the little plateau of the camp. Tiny, silky black and brown kids cavorted about the tents; a group of tall, lean handsome men wearing old uniform jackets, white turbans and loose white robes, gathered round. Most of them carried rifles and bandoliers full of brass cartridges. A white-bearded old man with a lined, dignified Old Testament face, carried his grandson, who was sucking a piece of sugar-cane. Women and girls, in faded chaudris and dirty-gaudy dresses, tousled and barefoot, grouped about their infants and children. The reigning matriarch came up; she had a child in her arms, one in her belly (which she patted demonstratively), cherry-red robes, loads of silver bangles and chains, a gilt necklace, a 'ruby' in one nostril, a gold ornament on her forehead, dark hair in small plaits, healthy red-brown skin and a wide laughing mouth. A man's zip-fastened cardigan slightly diminished the effect. She invited us to her large, open tent whose striped rugs hung over the frame to air. Inside, we squatted on carpets, leaning against cushions or hassocks, by the hollowed, charcoal hearth while water for tea was poured from a tin-plated copper pot. The support of these 'houses of hair' was a single huge curved beam held in position by a stout prop. Old slack-breasted women crouched round the edges. Rifles and a radio were prominent, a lamb's carcass was drying on a hook. It was a friendly, itchy half-hour, among the kids and sheepskin rugs and fleas. Before we left all the men, and after much cajoling, all the women except the old grannies, formed groups for photographs.

The road to Herat follows the river course, rising slightly above 3,000ft among sandstone hills with views of a jagged mountain range, the Paropamisus, to the north. There were tufty growths of emerald-green grass among the purple, sage-brush scrub where camels grazed; a great windmill tower used for grinding grain heralded a solitary village. This country of the Timurids—the post-Mongol invaders of Persia under Timur-i-Leng (Tamerlane)—still remains as wild and empty as even 'overlanders' could wish, leading south, to the Desert of Despair. Sections of a newly laid rail-track and raised permanent way, with heavy American equipment, foretell the pattern of the future.

Treelined avenues, fir, spruce and oleaster act as radii to the central square of Herat, providing an approach worthy of a town founded by Alexander. From one side to another they extend five to six miles. We approached out of the desert suddenly, with a right-angled turn at a petrol station, then a gradual descent past the seven isolated minaret towers, so like giant factory chimneys at a distance, with relics of grape-blue mosaic and panelled decorative bases, which dramatically straddle the road. Under the trees stalls cluster along the 'jube' until the avenue debouches into a wide, dusty square. Open-fronted carpenters' shops, grocers, tea and spice merchants, furriers—a full-sized leopard skin for $75—fruiterers, sweet shops, tea-shops (chai khana) where sitar and drum music can be heard, shops selling bul-buls, crowd in on all sides. Traps for hire are ranked, sparkling in the sun, or dash up the street enveloped in yellow clouds: the horses have bells, coloured tassels and bead ornaments; the cabs much brass-work, bright plastic and gay bobbles.

Women with jewelled nose-rings carry babies with heavy eye make-up. Tall, dignified, aloof but courteous men, with dark beard and brow pass by in their loose pyjama-like trousers, shirt-tails worn outside, long cloth jackets of darker colour and white, blue, green or turquoise turbans—nowadays made of nylon net —wound round a small embroidered or gold-threaded skullcap. One splendid eagle-nosed old man welcomed us with generous gestures to join him at tea: it came in tiny Japanese pots and sea-green, blue-patterned bowls.

Herat, ancient Aryana, in the tenth century first city of Afghanistan, was a junction of trade routes to all parts of Asia, 'gate to India', and a fifteenth-century centre, in the Timurid renaissance, for art and culture. 'The whole habitable world had not such a town as Herat: it was filled with learned and match-less men. Whatever work a man took up, he aimed and aspired to bring it to perfection,' noted Babur, first Mughul emperor in the sixth generation after Timur. It is still an important market, with a main bazaar (formerly a tunnel) two miles long, now mainly stocked from Russia, and in appearance it is largely un-spoilt. The great buildings of the Musalla, with mausoleum, mosque and originally madraseh, erected by Gohar Shad, Tamer-lane's daughter-in-law although in ruins, dominate the place; the Friday mosque remains magnificent. Its beautifully proportioned courtyard held for us the last of a lovely bluish evening light: swifts dipped in flight among its arcades and four ivans; the high rectangular façade of the main ivan and two massive towers shone with mosaic. It had the embracing and friendly air of a lived-in place: children trotted across its court with their school-books, a mullah sat by the square pool; in an anteroom workmen were making star-shaped moulds for mosaic repairs. A green formal garden surrounds one entrance arch, through another we returned from cool, gracious retreat to the dust-hazed turmoil of the town. Three visits to Herat have not nearly exhausted its delights—among which is a terraced ruin of gardens. Takht-i-Safar, 'the travellers' throne.'

From Herat to Kandahar a sealed road, Russian-engineered, made speed and the passing scene more agreeable. Beyond the

long tree-lined southern avenue and some modern buildings, including a motel, we entered stony desert. Alkali flats or
bituminous outcrops stretched to a far horizon of contorted rock.
The illusion of seeing the actual curvature of the earth's surface
was conveyed by the road's endless endeavour to reach the edge
of a plateau, which as constantly disappeared to the fringe of
more identical knife-edged ridges. This pattern of the old sea-
bed plain and upthrust of unglaciated rock recurs from Turkey
to Turkestan. A few caravans of nomads (Kuchis), their carpets,
bedding, lambs, kids, infants piled on camel or donkey back,
their flocks of goats and sheep driven slowly ahead and chivvied
by white dogs, were the only signs of life. Dwarf red tulips
(Tulipa Praestans) occasionally surprised the eye in a scene of
dust, willy-willies and mirages of trees, water and sand, where
telegraph poles strung out singly across the vast emptiness,
seemed the very attar of desolation.

The route through this barren wilderness veered gradually
south-east, losing height until it reached the river Arghandab,
where real green water-meadows, fronded willows and fir-tree
shade seemed like a dream in the growing heat. Here were wayside
cemeteries of heaped stones and upright slabs, wells with shade
roof and wooden windlass wheel. A dusty brown owl sat by one.
After several such green belts at river crossings we entered the
double avenue of trees, shading road and sidewalks, past shrines
hung with green and red banners, that leads to Afghanistan's
second largest city.

An Afghani bus, 'that exotic and unusual creation of man, the
outside gaily painted with colourful scenes of rural life, floral
decorations, erupting volcanoes', preceded our entrance. It is
fundamentally a cattle truck, with high sides, a flat roof with
wooden rails to contain the baggage, and ten-inch boards fixed
across inside as benches, but no gangway. It stopped and started
for men to swarm over each other from roof, running boards and
interior and heave down their bedrolls and bundles. Then the
warm, phlox-scented, frog-croaking, dust-softened streets of Kandahar offered a taste of a more exotic East. Turbaned figures sat
cross-legged in kerosene-lit stalls among bright bolts of cotton and

silk, strange fruit, fly-blown meat and piled groceries. A man sat on the pavement grinding salt; a courtyard exhaled the breath of bakers' ovens. Henna-stained girls held out begging bowls, a teenage boy walked stark naked along the pavement past prim schoolgirls with satchels. Women washed clothes and babies and vegetables in a green backwater. There was strong bright sun, gay colour, dung and flies.

At dusk the bazaar provided a series of pictures—hurricane lamp or candle-lit scenes in which the chiaroscuro heightened the gleam of white turbans, white beards, bright cotton shawls thrown over a shoulder, where the shopkeeper still sat cross-legged among his sacks and heaps of grains and spices, his boxes of nuts and biscuits, beads, razor blades, bright red boiled eggs and embroidered caps. And among the potholes silent, lightless bicycles flitted up and down, tongas passed with a sudden rush of wheels. Stars looked down from the deep blue darkness over the great tiled gate arch to the bazaar and council court. We had rooms at the Khyber Hotel, a pull-up for long-distance coaches, and 'truckies', popular, it seemed, among hitch-hikers and some of those on the 'hash route'. Truckle beds, three or four to a room, bright pots of phlox and a communal shower with hole-in-the-floor convenience—cost 30 Afghani ($£1 = 170$Afgh). Against advice two of us dined in a local eating-house. Saucers of meat, spinach, potato, a plate of rice, chapatti and tea, were brought from a dim, smoky back room and carefully served on a spread table-mat; the meal came to 15 Afgh each. It was kindly set out, appetising, romantic, but for two days afterwards I regretted it!

As the city woke again to life in balconies and at washing places, we sped down another wide, double avenue with the Afghan hills standing clear as cardboard cut-outs in crisp air and limpid sunshine, northward now for Kabul. The concrete and asphalt highway, this time American-built, follows the course of the Tamak river for long clear miles; occasional green wadis and fortified villages break the uniformity of a road that resembles a metal tape-rule, diminishing with its dwindling telegraph poles to an unreachable horizon. Blue sky, sailing white cloud and distant jagged, snow-streaked mountains indicate an altitude of between 6,000 and 7,000 feet. At 'tea-stop' in Shahjni the small square was full of picturesque figures who squatted round in a sea of turbans, open waistcoats, knee-length shirts, as surprised to see us as we should be to see them at a wayside pull-up in Britain. More surprising to us was to see these same rough-hewn truck-drivers and herdsmen stop wherever they happened to be at sun-down, climb out of truck or bus, wash in some sandy puddle, unroll a rug and then prostrate themselves with forehead touch-ing the ground, before kneeling in lengthy prayer with faces towards Mecca.

Ghazni, seat of sultans and dynastic centre in the tenth century, lies a little back from the road, crowned by a virtual acropolis. Its castle walls cling with such tenacity to the cliff that it is difficult to tell where one begins and the other ends. They once served the purpose of fortress for Mahmud son of the founder of the Ghaznevid empire and known as 'the Image-Breaker' for his raids into India and spoliation of Hindu temples. Nearby, in open country, stand the remarkable 'Towers of Victory', a pair of octagonal star-shaped stumps, reduced now from over 200 to 70ft in a rich toffee brick tinged with red and decorated with carved terra-cotta. Their eleventh-century in-scriptions in Kufic lettering, celebrate Mahmud and Masud. They are surpassed only by Delhi's victory tower, Qutb Minar, 238ft.

Fortified hill villages occur more than once as the road climbs through the Desert of Top to the final plateau. From the far edge of the plateau one gains a first view of part of the 400 mile long mountain barrier that stretches almost from central Afghanistan to Kashmir: the majestic Hindu Kush. As we watched for fresh glimpses of this historic bulwark between central and south Asia, camel trains began to pass by; there were horses and traps on the farm roads, fields with winding lanes appeared, there were zig-gurat-shaped kilns and large estate enclosures in the widening out of a more populous, prosperous valley. Turbaned road-menders in ex-Army greatcoats, of World War I descent, stood back to watch the MCW as it entered the long, bazaar-bordered road that swings suddenly through a gap between craggy hills to con-

Page 125 : (*above*) Temple guardians at Kathmandu; (*below*) musician at Amber

Page 126: (left) Women weaving at Bhadgaon; (right) Newar tribes-women

front the dense agglomeration of Kabul.

Gateway to India, pivot of the old Silk Road to China, oasis city of the Hindu Kush, Kabul is one of the most individualistic capitals. Travellers still feel excitement at arriving there. A fertile plain at some 6,000ft bordered by a delicate blue lake in a mist of poplars, is dense with earth-coloured houses and streets of old wooden shops, splashed here and there by blue domes of mosques, new white buildings or grey roofs of barracks, college and palace, and enclosed by two jagged ridges over which great walls fling themselves above the fortress of Bala Hissar, where the amir lived up to this century. The turbulent, yellow-grey Kabul river cuts through the city centre—formerly enclosed by the three-mile circuit of walls and entered by seven gates—and in brilliant contrast a white ring of 16,000ft peaks, over which clouds mass to add height and purple shadows, closes in the whole north-west and north. It is a tribesman's city, the wild Afghans' Mecca, with a somewhat barbarous squalor in the narrow mud alleys and congested bazaars, but a Nordic air in the clean spacious streets and avenues, the tree-lined embankments and canals, the massive stone buildings of the centre, much of whose layout is German-inspired. A series of circular parks, an oval sports stadium, the grounds of the old white and gold palace, provide variety and 'lungs'.

Walking through the riverside bazaar of Kabul on Sunday one saw a city with a flower in its mouth—literally and as symbol. Men wore striped red and green, black and green, silver and black, or cream and brown 'chapans', a summer dust-coat with wide sleeves left to flap loose; many carried a rose between their teeth or held to the nostrils. (Afghans are all rose-lovers: some even sport them in the barrel of a rifle.) A rider in white robes and green turban on a white charger caparisoned in scarlet cantered up on tight rein, then sprang off with a flourish to greet a friend. Old white-bearded, white-clad patriarchs with gold-capped turbans shook hands or embraced, then squatted in groups to chat outside the Friday mosque. Well-scrubbed country boys, slant-eyed children and a few matrons in grey-blue burqas or chaudris of softly coloured silk, 'sun-ray' pleated from the neck

H

down, mingled with the younger women in modern open-work stockings, tight skirts and blouses. Chiefly it was a male parade, of hillmen and town elders and soldiers walking with linked arms. There were cucumber and cheese stalls on the river bridge, spices or pink and yellow 'kali', bright red hard-boiled eggs, sellers of iced raisin-water, fortune-tellers with astrological tables to make horoscope amulets, harness and brocade stalls. Donkeys staggered under great round panniers of oranges or apricots—Afghan sun produces some of the best fruit in the world—beggars squatted in a heap of multi-coloured patchwork rags. Over the balustrade of the riverside were hung dark red rugs and carpets for sale. Bursts of sitar music came from the 'chai khanas' alongside. There was pride, humour, vitality in the faces of the throng, whether they were brown-eyed or of Aryan blue, grey- or henna-bearded, or red in token of having made their pilgrimage to Mecca.

In the green outskirts of the park men were wrestling, Cumberland-style, with backers and tipsters squatting within a ring formed by tribesmen and soldiers. Excitement ran high with each round of falls. Nearby a stall offered target practice—shooting a marble off a stick at five or six yards with painted airguns—and later a political meeting got under way. A throaty orator perched precariously on a tiny platform under a red banner: his supporters, some in the branches of trees, cheered the regular 'punch lines' in his rhythmic harangues in deafening unison. The meeting only dispersed when a dust storm blew up, and then turned to heavy rain with forked lightning flashing against snow-and-mist shrouded hills. March and April are the two rainy months.

The enclosed bazaar on the right bank of the river, a series of open arcades with central fountain and wooden upper gallery, surged with people. Cloth merchants, in their good suits and karakul caps, undercover money-changers, cotton and silk retailers, tea-blenders, spice merchants and corn dealers conducted their trade here. With mock circumspection, sundry looks round and fingers laid to noses, one entered a gallery shop to examine suit-lengths, enjoyed a bowl of green tea and a sweet biscuit with the merchant and came out with Afghanis at a slightly better rate to dollars or sterling than elsewhere (£1= 178A). The air of secrecy added spice to a deal whose main advantage lay on one side—the merchant's.

Further up, beyond the second river bridge, a whole street was devoted to furriers and curio dealers. One could buy a German porcelain coffeepot, an antique blunderbuss, an Alexandrian tetradrachma, a silk embroidered Chinese robe or carved lapis lazuli seals. The stimulus to buy antiques in Kabul comes partly from the museum, whose collection of coins, ivories, images and Greco-Buddhist sculpture is first class. The caves of the Buddhist monks and the gigantic Buddhas—whose legs Nader Shah caused to be broken—carved in the cliffs of Bamian are a major attraction of the Chardels Pass through the Hindu Kush, also in this challenging area.

The other bank of the river is lined with lock-up shops, jewellers, chapan sellers, bakers, herbalists with drugs and seeds in old gin and whisky bottles, 'cupboard-shops where the merchant is tucked away among his canes of sugar wrapped in brilliant paper, his furs, knives, striped rugs, long-necked bottles, fat-bellied pots, his books of large squiggly lettering, his silver bracelets and gold-embroidered caps' and in most of them a cage or more of minute singing birds. Behind, in the congeries of muddy lanes, tinsmiths and boot-makers, butchers and skin-curers pursue their noisy/gory trades.

For our type of traveller Kabul offers variety of accommodation and food : from the Hotel Adriana on the outskirts—PLEASE SPEAKE SLOWLY warned a notice in the corridors—at 55Afgh per room, the newer Hotel Jamil near the bazaars at 80Afgh for room with shower or the more traditional and cheaper Jaweid (66Afgh), to the Kabul Hotel with luxurious double rooms from 300Afgh. The Kabul had a choice of table d'hôte lunches and dinners at 40 or 50Afgh : rice soup, braised tongue or ribs of mutton, potatoes, peas, carrots and chocolate mousse; the Jaweid à la carte, somewhat cheaper; or one could take a self-service meal in the Khyber coffee bar and restaurant, where the universal fish and chips and hamburgers were served to travellers of all types in beads, jeans, birds' nest beards and poshtins.

On the last morning some of us rose at 5 am—with the
sun—to climb one of the bare hills that encompass the city. The
dust road leading away from the river, beyond the Shah-do-
Shamshira mosque, was deserted at this hour. It narrowed to a
rocky lane—an alley or midden between the piled-up mud houses
—then came out on to quarry waste and scree until it reached a
sharp ridge. The going was steep, open to the icy winds of early
spring and, when we reached the summit at about 6,000ft,
spectacularly rewarding. The great valley basin spread its secrets
at our feet—airport, palace, river, green and white mosques,
straight-ruled streets with their ranks of stalls, surrounding green
paddies, Alexander's well, the blue lake and the road back to
Ghazni visible through the tawny Afghan hills. Buzzards
wheeled overhead, a few bright anemones and lizards hid among
the boulders, but what magnetised our gaze was the glittering
white splendour of the Hindu Kush, with outlying peaks barely
thirty miles away. We looked out towards those legendary places,
Balkh, 'mother of cities', Samarkand, Mazar-i-Sharif, by which
Genghis Khan, Tamerlane, Babur had gone to found empires
from India to the Aegean, and in bringing the nomadic energies
of Central Asia within the orbit of Persian civilisation had pro-
created more than one artistic renaissance.

When we left from the square by the Khyber restaurant, where
workmen squatted against the wall to relieve nature before going
to work, and then turned up the riverside road, a stock market
was starting. Cattle, horses, camels were hobbled and penned on
the brown earth opposite the slaughter-house: teams of coolies
strained and heaved at solid wooden carts loaded with a ton of
meal sacks; rough drovers looked the part of wild hillmen; a
company of army recruits swung by with hard, impassive looks.
The rough vigour of leaf-brown and leather-brown faces accorded
with Afghanistan's history of invading hordes and fierce tribal
wars.

From a wide green rivage the Kabul river toils to enter the
jaws and relentless throat of a cliff-gloomed defile. It boils and
storms over boulders and rapids, past scree-shoots and water-
slides, roaring at one point down a thunderous fall into a caul-

dron pool some hundreds of feet directly below the road. Acute hairpin bends squeeze past towering rock faces, or pierce them by curved tunnels in a narrow ribbon of road at the mercy of rock falls. Sky is shut out by looming crags: golden eagles carve and quarter the upper air, the swings and zigzags of the route add to the vertigo of precipitous drops on the near side. Now and then a bedraggled camel train hugs the cliff face, its drivers thwacking the beasts to keep them out of traffic. Eventually the boiling waters cease to bubble and seethe, the river emerges from its iron confinement and the banks open out to the shores of a mirror-calm lake, an artificial turquoise-blue against sheer brown slopes. A gravel road comes in here crossing exposed hills and stony watercourses from Kabul, a camel and truck route to avoid the gorge. It is just possible for adventurous coach drivers when rock falls block the pass. Bob had negotiated it in sleet.

There is a village too of paddy fields and cow pastures, walled farms and waddling ducks, sweet-smelling groves of oleaster and pink-washed bungalows. In the wooden shanty shops turbaned tailors sit machining embroidered waistcoats, stalls sell dried fruit and porters' round padded caps. There are almond blossom, purple daphne, boy herdsmen in violet turbans. The place seems another Shangri-la of sequestered living. Lower down a great hydro-electric plant plant has been built: the river changes from brown to aquamarine, then to ice-green and rushes like soda-pop close beside the road, sometimes apparently flowing uphill.

The river's course continues to widen. More distant elephant-grey cliffs appear, some holed with cave dwellings, beyond smooth sand-spits and palm-tufted islands: herds of black buffalo wallow in the wide shallows; the feathery light green trees and long yellow grass give a feeling of Africa to the warm air. We are approaching Jalalabad, centre of Nangrahar province, altitude some 4,000ft less than that of Kabul: temperate even in winter, it lies on a pleasantly verdant plateau. We break for lunch at the Speenshaw Hotel and, after so many days of desert sand and rocky passes, are delighted to enter a lush green garden shaded by palms, curtain-figs, bottle-brush and tulip trees. The scents and blooms are those of an English June—snapdragons and stocks, wallflowers and hollyhocks, nasturtiums and geraniums, musk roses and orange-blossom. Mynah birds and bulbuls sing away in the bushes, hooded crows peck at the red-yellow flowers of the tulip tree. Already it is another world—a preface to India.

We negotiate the border post without fuss—*chai*, exchange of cigarettes with some of the hangers-on for rolled leaf 'bidis' or offer of 'hash' in a screw of brown paper—then, in mist and sharp showers of rain, we start the climb out to the Khyber. After a maze of valley road round crags, where yellow crocus and calceolaria, purple mezereon, comfrey, mullein and yellow-and-black henbane grow, we take up position in the queue of trucks, hoping not to be slowed by their stalling on the climb. The long, back-twisted bends swing in the dripping vapour sometimes as embanked shelves of hewn stone past waterfalls, rusted railway relics, almost inaccessible forts on every crest, past the roadside tablets and emblems of famous regiments and actions, past the road sign 'Camels only' for our highway's predecessor, up and out of the tangle of subsidiary hills and gorges to the breach in this sheer mountain wall and the great sandstone fortress of the summit, Shagai Fort, with the flag of the Khyber Rifles. Vultures wheel overhead. The pass rises to 3,500ft, only a minor elevation compared with others that we have crossed—'as passes go,' says Robert Byron, 'the Khyber is invitingly mild.' The complex of crags and savage hills, crowned by seemingly impregnable strong points, the uncompromising hostility of the terrain and the knowledge that conquerors and empire defenders, from the Aryans descending upon the Dravidians of northern Indian, the Persians under Darius annexing the Punjab to the Achaemenid empire, the armies of Alexander, the hordes of Genghis Khan, the Mongols, the Afghans, down to the British and sepoy regiments, held these numbered crests and forts to the last drop of blood and sweat—these make the impress of the Khyber.

A bazaar at the summit, half underground, offers colourful wares and sights. We were particularly intrigued by three young men walking self-consciously together in white robes and a sort

of black bowler hat with green streamers, to indicate descendants
of the Prophet. One can buy, it is said, any type of rifle here made
up from authentic parts, gleaned from the warring armies past
and present. Caveat emptor!

Afghanistan suited the travelling mood of the Sundowners : a
powerful, primitive landscape, towns and cities of individual,
unwesternised character, an independent virile people with the
bearing and manner of equals. A particular image recurs. We
came on a small clear stream running through desert sand scores
of miles from anywhere. A straggle of stunted thorn trees and
ruined mud-brick hovels led out beside it to a half-buried flour
mill. Its intact millstones, flour-dusty walls, store bins, beams
blackened by smoke from the firehole in the floor and a small
store of wood for charcoal suggested that it might still be used by
wandering tribes as a bakehouse. We stopped by the stream for
lunch and siesta. An Afghan bus pulled up and its passengers
obviously had the same idea. They fanned out alongside us and
the stream. 'Here at last', as Robert Byron remarked, 'was Asia
without an inferiority complex.'

# 5 ACROSS INDIA

*If I were an Indian millionaire I would leave all my money for the endowment of an atheist mission.*     Aldous Huxley

The run-down to Peshawar from Khyber is swift and exhilarating, with glimpses of the snow-clad heights of Swat and the Chitral range, of lilac hills, outlying forts and lounging Pathans. Handsome, fierce-looking and conspicuous in their baggy trousers, red velvet waistcoats and leather cartridge belts, they belong to the Kipling tradition: proud, but somewhat passé. Border manners soon change to the Pakistani mode. The plain becomes remarkably green, with willows and fresh spring foliage: the villages are crammed with people wandering across the roadway and slow-moving carts. There are hucksters, prayer-mats and the first signs of heat haze. We have the feeling of *déja vu*, of riding on a half-remembered highway into the British Empire, almost of re-entering the past. Any minute now we expect to see a solar topee.

At Peshawar, only 189 miles from Kabul, the impression is reinforced. We stay overnight at a dak bungalow, see lizards scurry into a corner when our charpoys (string and bamboo beds) are set up, enjoy again a dewy English garden with jasmine, roses, syringa, sweet peas, the flowers exiles planted still tended by the mali—and meet again a flush lavatory, instead of these smelly holes-in-the-floor favoured from Turkey onward. Only casually used, the bungalow has large dim rooms of cobwebby furniture. It could be taken for the scene of Kipling's tale of the haunted billiards' room. In the background three or four dazed Pakistanis struggle to produce thirty omelettes, teas and chapatti on two or three choked primus stoves.

Beyond the dak compound are the British garrison and colonial buildings, in the familiar Anglo-Indian Palladian style, with colonnades of creamy stone, served by red or grey dirt roads; and white bungalows with shutters, lattice screens, pillared porches and tiled roofs in neat walled gardens with eucalypts. Greyish-skinned clerks in grey suits go past on upright bicycles; cigarette booths, tongas and motorcycle cabs in dazzling colours spill over the road between the various ministry and regional offices. All is the same it seems, quiet, orderly—'time for tiffin' perhaps?—merely with the difference of national government.

Peshawar bazaars are the meeting places of people from everywhere. They crowd its 'Street of Storytellers' (not tales from the adventurers and caravan companies who used to camp there, but crowd oratory today), its 'Street of Singing Birds' (devoted now to shops selling brass and copper ware), its 'Street of Potters' and 'Mochilara', or Shoemakers' Street, where the Pathan 'chappal' are made, its 'Street of Dentists', where mouths in paint and plaster and the awful models of mouths magnified to the proportions of a nightmare gape and grin from the doorways. Afghans, Iranis, Afridis, Uzbeks are involved in endless bargains with traders over endless cups of green tea. Of Peshawar's secrets and sins, its hemp and cocaine, its parasites and money-changers, its eunuchs and male 'women', 'rouged, with eyebrows plucked and painted, with gold in their nostrils and ears', it is enough to say that it is the market, as well as the Paris and New York, of Central Asia.

Kingfishers and green parrots joined the vultures on the road to Rawalpindi. It was a green-gold-grey drive over a swimming, shimmering plain, past swampy farmsteads, red-soil plantations of rye and barley, bamboo crop and stock shelters, shady avenues of spruce and eucalypt, as far as the wide crossing of the Indus. The panorama of distant blue hills, the brown water and mud shoals with large islands of sand in the flood course, appeared African in scale and atmosphere. For the crossing at Attock below the junction with the river Kabul, 'the British had thrown a double-decker iron bridge, a lumpish powerful structure, rail-

way above, road below, with iron gates at each end to be closed
at night with chains and huge bolts and watchful sentries with
fixed bayonets' (James Morris : *Pax Britannica*). The place names
about here are Lawrencepore, Campbellpore and Prang. This
crossing-place for armies on their way to the forts and entrench-
ments of the Afghan frontier, and for Alexander and the Emperor
Akbar before that, is well defended and controlled. We waited
for military police permission to pass through the portcullis and
cross in single line : no smoking; NO CAMERAS.

Dust-patch village squares, roadside bathing and washing
pools, shade trees full of parrots and mynah birds, big, grey,
humped Brahmani bulls, wooden-wheel pumps in the fields,
heralded the country of Kipling's *Kim*. Small towns of stamped
mud streets were thronged with white robes, saffron turbans,
hanging shirt tails and spotted chadars, beautiful liquid-eyed
children, wandering cattle, dung and flies and dung. There was
the glimpse of an old mosque in oyster-shell scaled brick among
ramshackle streets or of a pink mosque in open country against
blue hills. Castor-oil plants grew by the road, a swallowtail
butterfly flickered past, lemon, green and black; in a field an old
man in clean white dhoti sat spinning grey wool. A double rain-
bow formed against thundery grey skies over a sultry, steaming
plain : it grew hotter, too hot. At length the coach stopped. We
had reached Rawalpindi.

The contrast between Islamabad, the spacious, gracious, unfinished national capital—to which one goes for embassy matters
—and Rawalpindi only a few miles away, is striking. In Islamabad dual carriageways, wide green verges, smartly functional
mosques and cinemas, white or pink villas with patios, Corbusier-
inspired embassy buildings, challenge the bright air and the red
hills with their 'new look' of national consciousness. Rawalpindi,
now headquarters of the Pakistan army, is made to seem ramshackle and seedy, especially at dusk. The bustle of cars, smart
youths in dark glasses and well-paunched businessmen at restaurant and 'drugstore' soft drink counter along the main thoroughfares, contrasts with the bazaar fringe—and the beggars. The
footless, those without arms or with only half arms, the sightless

led by milky-eyed children (suffering from trachoma), the crawler on elbows and knee pushing a begging bowl, the other leg twisted back behind his scrawny hip, the squashed dwarf with huge nodding head and contorted knees, less than half a yard high as he squats on a cloth between lighted candles, the man carrying his paralysed wife like a sack on his bony shoulders —these are the relics of Pakistan's 'old look'. In Murree Road a woman sits, veiled, head bent with her skinned-rabbit child resting naked on her thighs, mutely asking for its life : one of the faceless, nondescript, hopeless. Sometimes, a passing student looks back, hesitates—then hurries on.

We continued to the old provincial capital, Lahore. At the crossing of the river Jhelum, which flows down from Kashmir to join the Indus, baggage camels were mustering on the mud-flats, under the wall of an ivory white temple with delicate tracery and slender minarets looking across the sliding, beige water. The roads were wide, unshaded, the landscape green or scrub-coloured in the sandy foothills : bougainvillaea, jacaranda, hibiscus made splashes of brilliance. We crossed the Chenab, another Kashmiri tributary of the Indus. In the fields bullocks were at plough, wells were being dug out, women carried past their balanced loads, like a frieze of statues. A young boy, of beautiful delicate olive-yellow face, supported a great baulk of timber on his head. Bactrian camels transported vast sacks of fodder : their dung pats were quickly collected to stack in cones for fuel near houses. In one village square children swarmed round a snake-charmer and his hooded cobra, squatting half-naked in the dust, while their mothers, brilliant in saris or knee-length brocaded tunics and tight silk jodhpurs, shopped at the flimsy rush-mat stalls.

A jostling, shouting procession suddenly blocked our progress down a crowded street. A white horse, covered with garlands of flowers in gleaming harness with red tassels, went before a group of men who were beating themselves noisily on the chest with the flat of their hand; some, using chains or thongs laced with bits of metal, drew streams of blood from their bare backs. In the middle tottered an old, bearded ash-smeared fanatic. It was the tenth of

Muharram, the first month of the Moslem calendar and a day of mourning and self-mortification in which pious Shi'a Moslems recall the martyrdom of Hussein, grandson of the Prophet. Western eyes are not encouraged to observe the rites too closely. In Lahore several of our group had to be rescued by police with lathis, when their presence at the twelve-hour procession from the heart of the old city and through the bazaars was observed by an excited crowd.

In Lahore some stayed at the Park Luxury Hotel (at reduced rates), if only for its nostalgic imperial atmosphere. A cream and white colonnaded palace, built about 1890, with fretted stone cupolas lighted at night, embowered in lawns with feathery palms and flame-of-the-forest trees, it has suites of Victorian dimensions leading off corridors twenty-five feet high. Sitting-room, bed-room, bathroom—the bath a huge tub on legs in a tiled well—extend behind double screen doors from one balcony to another at the rear. Scarlet-uniformed bearers man the entrance to the foyer, all curio cabinets, red leather and brass-inlaid chairs in Mandarin style. Four great double swing doors lead to the dining-room, a discreet harmony of green walls, red plush carpet and green leather chairs, where waiters in white turbans, red-belted white tunics, and trousers ceremoniously serve the tables with their vases of larkspur under the great revolving fans. Chota pegs on the lawn, iced mango juice before breakfast. . . .

Others preferred the YMCA further up the Mall: separate-sex dormitories or single rooms at 5R50, and more like the Euston Road in its surroundings.

At the end of the Mall beyond the Victorian emporia with their original wooden fittings, stands 'Zam-Zammah on her brick platform, opposite the old Ajaib-Gher, the Wonder House'—in other words Kim's gun. The great green-bronze piece, Bangian Wali Top, cast in Lahore in 1761, ex-service in 1870, still dominates the road in front of the university, though 'who holds Zam-Zammah holds the Punjab' is best forgotten. The 'Wonder House' or museum (closed on Fridays) is worth more than one visit. Gandhara sculptures, bronzes of Vishnu and dancing Siva, a priceless 'Fasting Buddha' among many other Buddhas and

Bodhisattvas, Chinese porcelain and marvels of ivory carving, models of mosques and temples engross at least one afternoon; the Victorian room and its campaign relics with the adjacent display of Mughul watercolours, another. One or two items are uniquely charming—the thunderstorm pieces, in which prince and princess watch, from a canopied couch in a pink-walled palace, among white marble minarets and nervous-necked peacocks, for the frilly flickers of lightning and white swans to appear out of the massed, pitch-black cloud. Apart from hunting, war and love-making, 'looking at clouds' was a favourite pastime of Oriental potentates—for reasons which those who have waited for a monsoon to break will understand.

From the museum it is convenient to visit the Old Fort of Emperor Akbar, site of government for over eight hundred years. and the Great Mosque of Aurangzeb. Its walls and its fort are massive, seemingly ageless and part of the characteristic flavour of Lahore. The decorated arch of Alamgiri Gate, the elephant walk, the guns left by the British, the gardens with peacocks, deer and doves, the hall of mirrors—Shish Mahal—forming one side of the marble courtyard in Shah Jahan's apartments (Akbar built in red sandstone, Shah Jahan in marble), the baking heat on the parapets of this citadel, all are in the romantic convention. The camel lines and truck park under the walls, the hucksters' stalls and bicycles in ranks ten deep, a milling confusion of tongas, taxis, coolies, glimpses of the crumbling maze of alleys and shanties beyond the old gates, or of a bald Buddha-like figure on a shop balcony, placidly smoking a hookah, oblivious of all the frenetic turmoil and decay—these are redolent of 'the wonderful walled city of Lahore' known to Kim. Close by, in cloistered calm, a Sikh temple commemorates the 'Lion of the Punjab', Ranjit Singh, in glistening white stone; its gold-leafed dome and mirror ceilings, tricked out with coloured flowers of semi-precious stones, make a confection whose apogee is found in the Taj Mahal.

Badshahi Masjid, surrounded by lawns and gardens where old and young lie out in the shade, has oyster-coloured domes, and strawberry-sandstone minarets. Its great courtyard was too hot to cross with bare feet—shoes and sandals being with the

guardian of the door—and we hugged the shadow of the wall.
The fine painted arches and ceilings on the other side were our
reward, but it is the sheer scale of this building, the largest
mosque in the world, and its enormous onion-shaped domes that
one associates with the Mughuls, which last longest in memory.
As we returned to the Mall, past a very English white sandstone
Anglican cathedral of orthodox size, the immensity of Badshahi
came clear.

What is the flavour of Lahore? From the Mall, apart from its
angular babus riding angular bicycles, its squatting penmen and
'pan' sellers, or at nightfall, the tinkle of tongas in the warm
scented dusk and the corpse-like sleepers on the pavement or
decrepit charpoy, suddenly clearing consumptive throats with
jerky noises, it could be an amalgam of Bournemouth of-the-
four-star-hotel and Boscombe Road tattiness, of the neo-concrete
and the outworn Victorian. Until, that is, one has seen the
Shalimar gardens laid out in 1641. The road to them passes the
Zoo and the Presidency, and skirts a pleasant open canal, before
coming to a chaos of street stalls and tonga traffic. Once through
the gate one is in paradise, especially if the day is a holiday.
Brilliant begonias, petunias, zinnias, nemesia, African daisies,
roses, bougainvillaea with orange-coloured lianas, blue morning
glory surround and indeed emerge, on stone supports, from the
three long, terraced pools. They are linked by marble stairways
and lead to an old mosaic arch. The colour against the white
terraces, with a limpid blue sky and its reflections in the
pool is exquisite, but as nothing beside the colours of the pro-
menaders. Women, like gorgeous butterflies in their saris, or in
brocade tunics and satin jodhpurs, float along beside the pools:
small boys in shining tinselly costumes, with ruby and emerald
head-dresses and garlands of marigold heads, walk beside them;
babies in shawls and cloth of gold have black eye make-up.
Dandies parade in white, coxcomb head-dresses and snow-white
robes, each with a claque of followers. A tall stout man in long
snowy shirt and Turkish slippers is followed by three or four
servants to carry his tiffin-tin, his raised umbrella and his transistor. Hypnotised by the parade, we scarcely notice the dragon-

flies, the green parrots, the striped white and grey squirrels or the youths in pukka white flannels playing a cricket match on a corner of the shaven grass. This is Lahore's flavour—Shalimar's flight of exotic human butterflies and the equally popular Zoo's shabby sloths and black Himalayan bears, caged and crying.

A procession of pilgrims confronts us at the customs post, coming from the other side : stout grey grandmothers in pantaloons or sagging saris, bearded patriarchs in cream cotton nightshirts, trousers and yellow turbans. Sikhs with flashing eyes, bracelets, and beards kept in place by a bandage or hairnet, top-knotted boys with a handkerchief tied on their heads, kohl-eyed babies— and enough tin trunks, bed-rolls and tiffin-tins, carried by servants, to see them out of this world and into the next. They squat in family groups gathered in the shade of large coloured awnings, under the eyes of the gaitered, pouched and pipe-clayed police, or seek shelter by the lime and pseudo-acacia trees. It is a kaleidoscope of colour, bustle and noise—music blaring from loudspeakers, lianas of purple flowers hanging down over the hutted office, a police superintendent in blue shirt and navy shorts sitting behind a table in an open bamboo shelter, a small, dusty, ragged urchin—another Kim— in patchwork pants and wide grin scurrying for his pice as tea-boy (army tea of sugar, condensed milk and a handful of tea boiled up together in the kettle). Hoopoes roost in the trees and a warm breeze comes in languid puffs across the plain. The military strut by in their regimental blue and maroon puggrees, knife-edged khaki shorts and carefully parted brushed-up beards; a white-moustached old man pulls the cord of a punkah outside the interview room. The stallholder cooking potato cakes, soya-bean savouries and small, fluffy chapattis does a roaring trade. All feel a sense of occasion. WELCOME TO INDIA reads the notice at the far end of the series of barriers—and at about 3.30 pm, complete with our 'liquor permits', we pass the last one.

The road led between rye fields and pasture and by slow canals towards Amritsar. There were chain-and-bucket wells worked by a camel or bullock, oxen and camels yoked together to plough, white roadside shrines with yellow cloth-covered inner cells, heavy wooden-wheeled buffalo carts weaving along the crown of the road, blue jays and green parrots and flask-shaped weaver-birds' nests in the peepul trees, and falling across all the low rays of a brassy gold sun. The bony-hipped, big-horned buffaloes were led at sundown by small boys into muddy pools to wallow up to their nostrils after the heat and toil of the day. The dim glow of roadside smithies, the thin smoke of dung fires, the gleam of brass water-pots on the heads of women, the glare of lighted fruit and vegetable stalls in the villages, full of chillies and cucumbers, mangoes and bananas, the looming white shapes of wandering cows in a starry dusk changed to kerosene or neon lights in cycle shops and car body repairers, to tractor works and then to a rash of bazaar alleys and cab-lines, proclaiming Amritsar.

> The Golden Temple of the Sikhs is genuinely eighteen carat. It is also exceedingly sacred. Holiness and costliness make up for any lack of architectural merit. We went in barefooted—the Sikhs insist on this sign of respect. Picking our way among the bird-droppings and expectorated betel that strewed the cause-way, we advanced gingerly towards the most golden and holiest of the shrines which stands islanded in the middle of the sacred tank. In the holy of holies three magnificent old men were chant-ing ecstatically to the accompaniment of a small portable har-monium, which was being played with one finger by the fourth, yet more superbly patriarchal. (Aldous Huxley)

We also went into Amritsar's Golden Temple across the cause-way. Its doors are always open—symbol of the anti-caste system taught by early Sikh gurus. Three magnificent blind old men were still chanting, while a fourth played the harmonium and a drummer subtly varied the rhythm. A stream of worshippers came over the golden, balustraded bridge, knelt, kissed the threshold—or, after touching it with their right hand, pressed it to eye, head, lips, shoulders and heart—received the small 'plum' of sweet fudge in a folded leaf, then crowded into the sanctuary to hear the prayers which are recited continuously day and night. A sheet spread in front of the altar sagged with notes and coins and

Page 143: *(left)* Saddhu in Kathmandu; *(right)* in Durbar Square, Patan

Page 144: (left) Swayam-
bunath stupa; (right) art
and craft shop in Patan

flower-heads in return for the 'puja' or prayer offering. Some of the congregation ascended the marble stairs to the upper storey, with its flower-painted walls, mirror-inlaid ceilings and lovely mosaic embrasures, to make room for new worshippers and to watch the service at length. We climbed to the roof, whose domes and pinnacles are plated with gold. An artist in blue turban and white beard sat cross-legged on a small platform part way up repainting some of the panels with a fine brush : in alcoves, three priests sat on carpets reading aloud from the Granth, the Sikh holy book. From the roof we looked down over the sacred tank, at the black and white marble surrounds and the gilt-pinnacled outer temple. The whole gold and sugar-icing spectacle was a child's dream of heavenly palaces, redoubled and shimmering in the carp-teeming water.

In the sacred tank itself father bathed young son; heavy, white-moustached grandfathers took their leisurely dip, carefully closing mouth and nose, women had a special place for their sari-clad immersion. A near-naked saddhu, wreathed in marigolds and jasmine, with waist-length hair, trident and attendant acolytes, paced along the sides in meditation; another loin-clothed holy man, saffron shawl flung over one shoulder and brass alms bowl on a chain, stood in a trance; an emaciated pilgrim dozed against the wall, his long staff beside him. Bearded temple guards in blue turbans, long-sleeved white tunics, with halberds and short daggers in their scabbards, stood at the entrance gate. They were picturesque, genially smiling figures in the morning sun. Could they be the same in breed and belief as those 'dignified looking Sikhs, venerable in their long beards and wearing the bright blue turbans of the militant Akali sect', who were seen sitting cross-legged 'all along the platform of Amritsar railway station, each with a long curved sabre across his knees', waiting quietly at this last stop in India in 1947 to attack the next trainload of Moslem refugees trying to enter Pakistan? The museum of art within the precincts certainly had the most gory and explicit pictures of massacre, mayhem, decapitation, men sawn in half, among the memorable scenes from Sikh history back in Mughul times. The shops outside the temple gate were stacked with razor-sharp

I

kukris, sabres, swords and businesslike knives. And when they were emigrating to India, trainloads of Sikhs and white-capped Hindus ran a similar bloodthirsty gauntlet on Lahore station, the last on the Pakistan side.

We strolled back to the temple gate, through the chaotic streets, crammed with cycles, trishaws, tongas, cows trailing their dung, children, shoppers, women with cheekbones standing out from their faces like the hips of cows, men with empty blistered eyes opening bloody-red mouths to spit out gouts of betel juice, a pitiful procession with a small corpse on a trestle, stalls of spices, book-stalls, piles of unripened oranges and savoury cookshops, to the coach. The traffic policeman on his plinth stood out like a school prefect, a marvel of ineffective smartness among it all.

Through the fertile farmland of the Punjab now and down the Grand Trunk Road to Jullundur. Barley was being cut by sickle, resplendent peacocks stalked for pickings in the stubble, wandering bullocks, and women coolies carrying bullock droppings in circular baskets on their heads, were the new perils of driving. We had refreshers at thronged steamy Ludhiana—crushed sugar cane, fresh limes, ice and salt and pepper in pint glasses; then lunch in the roadside shade—cold chicken, bread, bananas, on which a flock of goats and their herds made sudden irruption out of nowhere. On through late afternoon and evening by Ambala, and so to Delhi. Emerald parrots perched on the toddy palms, bare-bottomed children swarmed round stagnant pools, red-turbaned drovers, father with son, sitting high on their great wooden-wheeled carts eased patient grey bullocks with black-painted horns gently homeward. (Bullock horns seem to be coloured by regions—sometimes both are green, or one green and one red, sometimes they are concentrically striped red, green and white.) Slowly the sun became an apricot ball and at a bridge over one of the irrigation canals cast a splendid golden light over the landscape, with reflections prolonged endlessly away to the reedy horizon. Darkness had fallen before the green and red signal lights of an airport twinkled ahead and, through the usual tangle of glowing bazaars and gharris pulled by horses thin as latch-keys we came to the Kashmiri gate of Delhi.

The YMCA Tourist Hostel is not far from Connaught Place, business centre of New Delhi. Built by Indian architects in western style, the hostel offers something of the same surprise as the buildings of Chandigarh, the modern, secretariat city designed by Le Corbusier. Its uniform, fan-cooled rooms with their individual balconies and open corridor looking over the central garden-court and pool cost us 19R (£1=24R) including English breakfast. The cheaper separate-sex YWCA and YM are almost next door.

Three of Delhi's main areas of attraction are within easy reach. A pleasant walk takes one into Parliament Street and up to Parliament House, with the great imperial Central Vista to India Gate just beyond. After King George V had announced the transference of India's capital from Calcutta to its old centre—Delhi's history goes back over 3,000 years—at a Durbar in 1911, Lutyens was engaged to build Viceroy's House, and Sir Herbert Baker the two houses of Parliament and Secretariat. Imperial Rome clearly set the style for this ambitious undertaking : the buildings and layout impress by their splendid scale, superb for the old viceregal pageantry superimposed on Mughul memories. Even the Mall and Whitehall take second place to Central Vista on Republic Day, when lumbering elephants in golden masks and hieratic paint, prancing Naga warriors from the far north, tribal folk from Madhya Pradesh, ceremonially precede the great concourse of celebrities, while overhead streak jet aircraft of the Indian Air Force trailing coloured smoke, and every tree and square yard of grass between the avenue and its parallel canals is dense with spectators.

In Connaught Place, with its central lawns and brilliant flame-of-the-forest trees with parrots, bee-eaters, coppersmith birds, busy life begins at 10 am, when the shops open. A triple-ringed circus of pillared arcades in white stone and peeling paint draws in radial roads from all parts. Connaught Place has unvaried interest as a morning promenade. In it lately-arrived tourists seek the American Express, those departing the BOAC, KLM or Air India offices; Indian ladies chaperone their daughters loaded

with gold-embroidered silks and jewellery, and they dally over
sari material or their orders of mango pickle from select grocers;
photographers and antique dealers fill their windows with curious
examples of art. Small boys waylay one : 'Change money, sah'b;
best rates' or 'You wanna nice girl, mister? Or a boy'?; a tiny
blind girl led by her brother is thrust forward to kiss one's feet
for alms. The plump dark-suited businessmen are aloof and im-
mune; suave Sikhs seek chance of meeting European females;
an old man squats on a corner, by the pornographic bookstall,
offering woven rush table mats, a dozen for two rupees : he slowly
unwinds a filthy twisted rag from his dhoti to hoard the money.
Pairs of young men in dark glasses take coffee or an ice at
Wenger's; the Kashmiri Government Art Emporium offers its
panoply of papiermâché, embroidery and wood-carving; the
Kwality restaurant offers more appetising fare—liver and onions
or fish mayonnaise; taxis whizz round and round on the shiny
tarmac; petrol fumes, joss sticks, scents of frangipani, rose and
keora and the susurration of saris assail the senses. Before the
morning is over everybody has met everybody else at least twice.

Apart from the central market behind Connaught Place, the
street bazaar down one of the radial roads has particular interest.
Here, beyond the Indian shoe and clothing stores, the ice-cream
parlours, European bookshops and shiny gift galleries, there is a
long row of open stalls kept by Tibetans. Calm, statuesque
women, full-gowned in brown, dark green or maroon with scarves
bound crosswise over their bodices, black braids of hair and warm
ivory faces, or their almond-fresh daughters, offer the relics that
refugees have been able to bring or craftsmen to make from
Tibetan sources. There are prayer wheels, smooth-worn brass
and copper Buddhas with parchment prayer rolls in the base,
wooden dolls and devil masks, silver-mounted harness, jade, old
silver coins showing mountains and dragons, fragments of marble
statuary, tankas (ikon-like pictures painted on cloth), necklaces
of polished pebbles, tigerstone spoons and polished turquoise—
mementoes both meaningful and desirable.

On another radial road a striking strawberry-pink and cream
structure dominates a small public garden. Odd-looking in juxta-

position to banks and insurance houses and cinemas it is like a double helter-skelter or perhaps a set of giant's geometrical instruments—which is what it is. Yantra Mantra, the observatory built in 1710 by Maharaja Jai Singh II of Jaipur, an amateur astronomer and town planner who corresponded with European scientists. He built four other observatories, including a far more elaborate one at Jaipur. This one has escaped the fate of so many ruins, which merely become children's playgrounds.

After Central Vista and Connaught Place, the next attraction —though historically it should come first—is the nucleus of Old Delhi and the Street of Silver, Chandni Chouk. Built wide enough for the processions of the Mughul Emperor Shah Jahan to pass through, when he planned to make this the greatest city of the north, it is richer in sights and sounds that evoke the East than any other thoroughfare. We spent two hot afternoons there to absorb them.

A betrothed boy of nine or ten, for instance, in turban and best suit, preceded by pipers and drummers was followed by a caparisoned white horse, with gold ornaments at ear, head and crupper, carrying a girl in long plaits through a side street of overspill stalls.

> 'Give her the anklets, the rings and the necklace,
> Darken her eyelids with delicate art,
> Heighten the beauty so youthful and fleckless,
> By the Gods favoured, oh, Bridegroom thou art'
>
> ('Indian Love' by 'Laurence Hope')

Groom and bride-to-be both seemed dumbly bewildered, but their parents and relatives made up for it with uproarious laughing and joking. Around them burgeoned the birth control clinics: 'RUBBER GOODS and medicine for BIRTH CONTROL', 'VARIETY, the family planning store', etc, now supplanted the old notices for 'SON BIRTH pills' and 'FREE FREE—Secret of Happiness from conjugal encounter'. Times have changed: a free transistor radio is now offered to family men who volunteer for sterilisation after their third—or is it second?—child.

After the silver shops came the stores of cotton and silk stuffs, the clothing shops, the display of durries and sheets and blankets, the ribbon and bangle stalls and proliferating students' bookshops, in which politics and engineering were only rivalled by sexology. A gaunt near-naked Saddhu, three white stripes painted on his brow to indicate a follower of Siva, stalked through the throng unheeded. Tibetans in brown robes, three-cornered straw hats with small bells, took their begging bowls from shop to shop leaning on long staves. Crowds flocked into a Sikh temple, open shops were papered with posters of Vishnu, Ganesh, Kali in glossy Technicolor, sacrosanct cows halted their incommodious bulk among the vegetable stalls; machinists sat bent over their Singer sewing machines under harsh naked bulbs : dignified old men in white pyjamas did their embroidery at shop fronts; cook-shops and druggists were kept constantly busy, confectioners crouched in greasy garments behind their brass trays of sweet-meats, tobacconists and betel-sellers hawked their wares; there was a Montessori school and back alleys of bakers and cobblers in the darkness, filth and fumes of Doré's London. Ceaseless traffic of bicycles, taxis, tongas, carts, scooter-cabs wove through all this with raucous cries of warning, but always patient good humour. It was part of the India that 'takes everyone for granted, be he a mad man looking at the sun or raving profanities, or a naked ascetic, or a frock-coated, striped-trousered European hiding his nudity in the rigid framework of civilised dress' (Mulk Raj Anand). This is one of the few countries in the world where nothing seems ridiculous—or time-wasting, 'a land full of fragile people clothed in cotton and moving sedately to their own mournful music.'

Among the narrow alleys alongside Chandni Chouk can be found some of the old city mansions, relics of Mughul Delhi, balconied inside and out, with hidden courtyards, heavily carved wooden doors and fantastic chandeliers. The Street of Silver is a façade to many surprises. Another is the tradesmen's market, beyond the copper and brassware shops at the upper end of Nai Sarak : here painters, joiners, plasterers wait to be hired with the tools of their trade laid out on cloths before them. About

fifty waited as we passed, some looking quite without hope. Even
the cartful of chanting children wreathed with flowers, on their
way to a temple ceremony with their Hindu God under its
tinselled canopy smothered in flower chains and orange dye, and
all pulled by two magnificent Brahmani bulls with bagpipe
accompaniment, could not break through their lethargy. Just
behind this market the real squalor lay—a dusty encampment of
so-called tents, from which ran black, naked, dirty-nosed children,
shrivelled old hags, their dry flesh wrapped against their bones,
and boldly flaunting tatterdemalion women, clutching and
squabbling for 'bakshish'. HUNGER STRIKE posters fluttered
from the telegraph poles and hoardings, 'Pharaoh's chickens'
(vultures) scavenged in the already scavenged garbage.

Overlooking the market and this dusty compound stands the
Jama Masjid mosque built by Shah Jahan between 1644-58.
Its huge courtyard and prayer hall is reached by broad flanks
of steps colonised by meditators and mendicants. The towering
minarets and onion domes reflect the opalescence of the evening
sky. Though the brownish sandstone, worn and whitened by
birds, the rolled prayer mats and vast empty spaces in the surrounding city turmoil have less obvious appeal than Badshahi at
Lahore, built by the Emperor Aurangzeb a generation later,
Indians consider Jama Masjid the most noble mosque in the
East. Next to St Sophia it is the largest in Islam.

Red Fort, Shah Jahan's other masterpiece, built to shelter his
marble palace and also regarded as the most magnificent building
of its kind in the whole of the East, has the advantage of wide
green lawns to set off its strawberry sandstone. The length of its
curtain walls and barbican, the mass of its lofty battlements, its
corner towers and citadel are breathtaking at first sight : they
occupy a larger area than the whole of Connaught Place. Here
better than anywhere else both the strength and delicacy of
Mughul building can be appreciated in the exquisite pavilions and
statements of uncompromising power. A slab of marble, so finely
carved that it resembles lace, forms a window in the palace : gold
poppies painted on each panel of the square-faced columns in
the Hall of Private Audience, where the Peacock Throne used

to stand; a wall and ceiling in blue and gold with a background
of ivory-coloured marble so that the room looks as if it had been
hung with richest Genoese brocade : these are bijouterie, perhaps,
rather than architecture, but to earlier eyes, according to an inscription over the outer arches of the Hall :

> If there is a Paradise on the face of the earth
> It is this, oh! it is this, oh! it is this.

The palace reminds one that the Mughul conquerors and their
architects were hillmen, devotees of gardening and hunting : so
in the heat and dust of the plains they evoked cool, cloistral
beauty with polished marble pavements, lattice-work and long
arcades : with mosaics resembling flower-beds, and windows cut
out in floral patterns of marble and where possible buildings
flanked or surrounded by a sheet of water to give cool tremulous
reflections.

In the evening a *'son et lumière'* spectacle within the Red Fort
walls represents its history and that of Delhi itself. As light played
over the various turrets and domes and towers, as the sound of
cavalry charges, the wild screams of assault parties, the tunes of
British regiments, the echoes of marching feet and the retreat
were relayed through the amplifiers—recalling both the Persian
invasion and the Mutiny year, when troops in the Red Fort
forced the last Mughul Emperor, Bahadur Shah II, to head their
revolt—this place of ferocious and heroic deeds seemed once
more to live. A local thunderstorm broke with timely effect as
part of the drama.

Already nights were hot and stuffy. Day temperatures averaged
95°F and the tatties—screen lined with aromatic grass sprayed
with water from earthenware pots by coolies, or nowadays a
sprinkler—were in use in the hostel courtyard. There was no
inducement to sleep. Instead we walked along the oleander-
scented avenue towards Irwin Road and at a corner found a
Sikh Temple. Shoes were cast, head coverings found, and a genial
elder conducted us in. Inside a young man attached himself,
explaining the images, the ritual and some of the religious beliefs.
That it was past midnight did not matter. 'Indians are great

talkers and they are ready to talk . . . with what is often incredible frankness. Indians are natural hosts and their hospitality can be overwhelming. In spite of its aura of exoticism India makes itself more accessible to travellers than most countries.' After a couple of hours we were inclined to agree: for a guest, like a saddhu, brings down blessings on those who make him welcome. . . . As the young man walked back with us a wayside, flower-decked niche still had its twinkling oil lamp and its devotee.

It was another hot day to be heading south into Rajasthan, first down Irwin Road and then Gurgaon Road, past the international airport. Women hand-winnowing grain in the harvest fields, or carrying double water-pots on their heads, looked in their faded orange, red or dusty green saris like scorched and wilting ears of corn. Camel trains plodded by in clinging clouds of ochre dust led by women blackened by sun. Peacocks glittered like jewels in the stubble: cranes, egrets, ibis, herons and sandpipers stalked in the shallow pools. The bucket-chain wells were being worked more and more languidly. Only the drovers, with dark red rope twists of turban and handsome moustaches, enjoyed a stir of air on horse-back above their sheep. (The Rajput turban, like bullock horns, varies in colour and also in size with locality: small and white near Jodhpur, then as one goes north towards Ajmer and Jaipur larger and redder to the climax of an enormous balloon of dark crimson muslin—then back again to normal.) We took tea-break near Alwar, at an old 'circuit-house' with cool, colonial portico, scented garden and an interior that might have been that of an abandoned Scottish highlands hotel. Then on through the game preservation areas of wooded hills, and rocky defiles, where lanes through scorching sandy fields led to mud villages crouched under red crags. Forts crowned the heights, white temples appeared among the feathery, laburnum-leaved trees, giant lizards basked on the rocks, old leper women held out their begging bowls by the roadside, as in a daze of steely grey heat, we drew up in the small, shadowed square under the palace walls of Amber.

Amber is a magic relic today. Capital of the Kachwaha Rajputs for nearly six centuries, until Jai Singh founded Jaipur in 1727, under the protective alliance of the Mughul Emperors Babur and Akbar, who found the Rajput princelings the only Indians whom they could not subdue, its early seventeenth-century palace, built by Raja Man Singh, looks on its great rocky hill like the enchanted castle of legend spellbound by its reflection in the lake below. 'Walls of China' crown the fierce ridges of the enclosing hills : towers and a huge fort hold the topmost height. Below, at their foot, a sleepy, half-ruined, creamy-stone town mingles its farms and stalls, its oil mill where the bullock, blinkered by leather goggles and a rag tramps endlessly round the revolving shaft, its wandering Brahmani cattle, naked children playing about the pump, its elephant-god 'stupa'—a pyramid of mildly erotic carving, its food shops and its pale marble temple, all in comfortable medley.

Up the long, hot cobbled slope to the deserted palace one can ride in the swaying howdah of an elephant. The painted beasts, all lozenges, stripes and circles of white, vermilion, green and orange, were being fed when we arrived; great trusses of straw, two hundredweight a day thrown up under their false tusks into the loose pink wet palates. Their musician played us the 'elephant tune', a series of delicate, haunting modulations and whispering echoes on a long bamboo instrument, strung with horsehair and wire, with a hide-covered sounding box and played by a bow carrying tiny bells. It would have charmed the weariest beast : tune and player are quite hypnotic, unforgettable by any who visit Amber. . . . We sweated up the slope on foot through the vast stone arch and into a bare, sandy courtyard with a tree and spring of water, where jasmine and marigold garlands were sold by the yard to celebrants going to the temple of Kali.

The royal palace is approached by a long flight of stairs and a double gateway, after which all leather, shoes, sandals, bags, camera cases are left, before one may pass the massive silver-plated doors and marble facings of the temple. The doors stood open : a deafening cacophony of drums, pipes and clanging bells emerged; we were pressed forward by the crowd and, like other celebrants, received the 'bread and wine' (a ball of sweet fudge and raw spirits poured into the cupped hand) and the red spot on our foreheads. . . . The second courtyard contains the Hall of Public Audience, built of grey marble with sandstone pillars and elephant brackets to support a voluted roof. A further portal, Ganesh (Elephant) Pol, with a picture of an elephant at a sumptuous banquet, leads to the inner court of royal apartments under Bengali roofs grouped round a flower-garden. Ceilings and walls combine delicate mosaic with glass inlay: those of the women's rooms in the 'Zenana' are lined with slightly curved fragments of mirror, so that every movement is reflected in a thousand miniatures. In the dark, a single candle gives the effect of multitudinous starlight, and the image of the outside world has a glint like the curved highlight in an eye. Outer windows with stained glass pictures of flowers or miniature landscapes, and flower paintings on the walls, complete the adornment of this exquisite specimen of Rajput architecture. From the turrets one can survey the whole timeless enclave of Amber, its great straddling wall, its lake and gardens far below and, in a gap of the hills, Jaipur city.

A crowd had gathered in the sandy courtyard when we descended and with it a sudden hush. As we drew near a bright blade flashed in the air and a black goat was beheaded for Kali, its head falling on the hot sand. The sacrifice seemed to belong not here in the sharp sunlight, but to the Vaishnav temple lower down, entered by a marble 'toran' or elephant gateway. Here on a pallet in a recess of the red-painted walls, before a shrine blackened with ghee and smeared with 'kumkum' powder, the tousled guardian slumbered on through the afternoon in dirty loincloth and musty, incense-heavy darkness.

Jaipur, surrounded on three sides by rugged hills, lies only seven miles south-west of Amber, but the change of personality is complete. The best example of a planned city in India—not excluding Chandigarh—it was laid out in regular blocks, cut into six equal portions by paved streets over a hundred feet wide and intersected by narrower streets, unlike the usual town which so often appears to have grown up haphazard clustered along

cow-paths. A crenellated wall, some 20ft high and 9ft thick, enclosed the whole, pierced by eight gateways with kiosks and fancy
white designs resembling the paper-lace on a chocolate box. And
this capital, designed by Maharaja Jai Singh, after examining
the plans of European cities and studying Hindu treatises of
architecture, is all in terra-cotta pink. Its gates, its walls, its
palaces, its elegant baroque houses with their latticed windows,
are suffused with a colour which at sunset glows like the heart of
a rose. 'Pink is the blue of India.'

The city prides itself on modernisation—elegant hotels and
offices, western-attired businessmen, the latest automobiles; the
contrast provided by the people who have come in from rural
areas with traditional manners and habits is striking. Close beside
the Hawa Mahal, the Hall of the Winds, an extravaganza whose
broad, pink pyramid façade towers above the bazaar, we saw a
'Food Restriction Day' procession— a group of silver and wood-
wind bandsmen playing jazzed-up marching tunes, followed by
women carrying on their heads trays of food, sweetmeats and
fruit. A beggar in half a shirt lay dead in the gutter at nine in
the morning and was still there at two in the afternoon with flies
thick on his eyes, mouth and anus. A brick-red 'God', exactly
like King Edward VII, peered from a plaster shrine smothered
in offerings of coins and flowers. A skeleton of a man in a loincloth shuffled in the middle of the traffic on one shoulder and
his buttocks pushing a begging bowl before him. White-cockaded,
white-uniformed, blue-and-red turbaned police walked down
between the traffic lanes. The shops sold phallic symbols (lingam)
in gilt and painted marble, while pavement stalls offered gaudy
romances, erotica and Indian pin-ups; dignified white-bearded
merchants were sitting in their shop-fronts, naked paupers slept
under a banyan tree; ancient victorias and four-wheeled cabs
resembling sections of old third-class railway carriages rattled
past among camel-riders, elegant horsemen and muscle-straining
trishaw peddlers; flower-sellers squatted over masses of yellow,
white, rose and gold 'malas'—scented garlands for 25p each (less
than 3d); tribeswomen carried loads on their heads with the
bearing of princesses, with heavy 'slave' bangles clashing at their

ankles. And over all was the odour of joss-sticks and spices, cow-dung and urine, rich ripe fruit and jacaranda blossom, and the scurry of red-brown monkeys along the house-tops.

Jaipur's contrasts are unending. Two or three years ago the Maharaja of the State, owner of twenty forts and palaces and 83,000 acres of farmland, ran forty-five personal cars, from Bent-leys, Cadillacs and Rolls to Fords, Jeeps and Morrises. His palace occupies one seventh of the whole city area. Within a stone's throw of the palace a reeking alley, black and lightless at night, houses whole families in hole-in-wall dwellings : naked infants are laid out to sleep on a hand-cart, a young girl lies on a stone step, grandmother on an old trestle under filthy awning. In these cavernous holes barbers, bakers, cobblers, millers follow their trade. . . . India's mixture, beauty, fragility, decay.

The observatory, Yantra, in the palace compound, is a marvel : a great quadrangle filled with abstract sculptures, zodiacal dials, huge quadrants, instruments like giant launching-platforms for space rockets. Yantra Samrat or Prince of Dials, rises 100ft into blue sky. All are formed from twists and curves of grey and white marble set in red sandstone or pale yellow-washed plaster, and designed to measure local time, local latitude, eclipses and the sun's altitude and azimuth. From that scientific tour de force one goes out into the streets again, thronged with ruminating bulls, fakirs, garish doll deities, blind and acting-blind beggars, women feeding feeble infants from breasts like old leather bags, Brah-mans, the gutter-dead. These are the streets once supplied with trottoirs of hewn stone, central carriage drives, stand-pipes for water, tramways for rubbish collection and cast-iron lamp-posts by the State's British Superintending Engineer, Colonel Jacob.

From Jaipur eastwards to Bharatpur, Rajasthan showed its colourful best. Out through the wide bazaars, past the elegant terra-cotta façades, the single-storey almshouses for some ex-Shah's womenkind, we continued through Galta, where terraced tanks and creamy stone pavilions crowd into a picturesque gorge and a temple dedicated to the Sun God crowns a ridge, and then into sandstone hill country levelling out into an upland plain. Peacocks, jays as bright as kingfishers, green parrots, grey tree monkeys dodged among the dappled shadows of the neem trees; whole families were at work in the harvest fields, camels were hauling up the leather buckets of the wells, gangs of women half-heartedly mended the roads. Crazy cyclists suddenly swerved out and across the road a couple of yards in front of the speeding coach, missing by inches. In a village square disciples sat under a banyan tree round a holy man with gold-barred forehead, shaven head, orange robes, begging bowl and long, crook-handled stick. Lithe girls carried red earthenware water-pots carelessly balanced on their heads. India, still 99 per cent villages, where for tourists the sense of discovery remains more than in most places in Asia, offered curious and tempting sights on all sides. But when the steely sky of afternoon presses relentlessly down and the glare strikes one like a savage salute, such landscape becomes colourless, almost suburban.

Fortunately we came then to Fatehpur Sikri and its dak bungalow. Ordained by Akbar as his capital in place of Agra—Sikri being a village whose holy man had successfully prophesied to him the birth of an heir—the palace of Fatehpur Sikri took nine years to build in hard, weather-resisting red sandstone. After being occupied for seventeen years it was deserted, almost overnight, for lack it is said of an adequate water supply. The court was moved again, to Lahore. Akbar briefly revisited it once and so, over a century later, did Mohammed Shah when he was crowned Emperor of India. As a result, after all the intervening years, it is not a ruin but a well-preserved palace within the seven miles of its city walls, completely empty save for jackals.

Ascending the great range of steps to the Gate of Victory, we looked across a vast coral courtyard in which the mouldings, finials and sculpture were still clean-edged and sharp; no crumbling decay, no blurred outlines. The covered mosque beyond, divided into three square chambers, is particularly fine, both in proportion and detail : its delicately fretted screens are each of one piece of marble; the vaulted canopy of the cenotaph is mother-of-pearl; the Hindu ceilings supported by tall Hindu columns underline Akbar's taste and imagination in employing indigenous styles. The tomb of the holy man of Sikri is of blindingly white marble set among all the red sandstone. The Hiran Minar, a 70ft high shooting tower, is decorated with some tusks as memorial to Akbar's favourite elephant. The emperor's dining-room in the zenana is a charming oblong room with deep niches carved in the walls in which dishes were placed. One looks for a bright turban, listens for a light footfall—but in these rosy-red courts, in the Mint and the Treasury, the Baths, the Bedchamber and the remarkable special audience chamber with its ornate central pillar that spreads out at the top like a tree, as in the rose gardens outside, or away to the great boundary walls of the city in the flat khaki landscape there is just silence and emptiness. Only near the entrance children wheedle for bakshish, touts sell postcards and peacock fans, old silver rupees and East India Company quarter annas and a lean man in a yellow loincloth offers to dive from the top of the gate, eighty feet, into a narrow well hardly visible below.

To Agra, Akbar's earlier capital, it is twenty miles. When the sun has passed its height we leave the shady lawns of the bungalow, and cruise through torpid villages and hyacinth-choked pools to reach its environs before the swarm of cycles, gharris and trishaws fans out from office, shop, college, 'godown' and railway yard. The bazaars—medieval Kinari Bazaar and the winding lanes that take off from it—are celebrated for traditional handicrafts, embroidery, silk work, carpet weaving, leather and enamel work, which Agra has preserved in a progressively machine age.

After seeing the Taj Mahal from a train Kipling vowed never to go near the spot in case a closer view might break the spell. It is claimed to be perhaps the most beautiful building in the world. We went towards sundown, past circuit house and colonel's lodge, aflame with laburnum and bougainvillaea, down the gentle oleander-scented slope where trishaws and gharris deposited their silken-sari loads, and into the Indian crowd at the precincts.

From the entrance hall, where Lord Curzon's ornate lamp twinkled like clustered fireflies, we looked across cool water, cool tree-shade blue with jacaranda blooms, to crystal fountains and an emperor's dream in milk-white marble, framed in palms and cypresses, flawlessly mirrored in a long pool. To the flocking local visitors the Taj spelt grandeur, glory, grace, romance. Built by Shah Jahan to enshrine the remains of his beloved wife, Mumtaz Mahal, and constructed in every phase of the work by specialists, its great central dome within four smaller domes is flanked from the corners of the terrace by four slender minarets. The Shah and his wife lie buried side by side under the central dome, where light filters through a double screen of perforated marble. The terrace looks out across the river and upstream to Akbar's palace fortress, from which Shah Jahan, kept prisoner there for his last eight years by his usurping son Aurangzeb, could see the building dedicated to his consort's memory.

The shrine took twenty thousand workmen in daily employ fifteen years to build and cost the equivalent of five million pounds. To some, its fabulously expensive detail is as impressive as the vast dimensions and meticulous proportions of the whole : to others : 'It is made of marble. Marble covers a multitude of sins.' From the inlay of the perforated screen enclosing the ceno-taph and the marble of the tomb, fine enough to show a torch's light through its two-inch thickness, to the dado which runs round the mausoleum, everything is done with jeweller's finish. The flowers of the dado, bluebells, daffodils, tulips, crown im-perials, lilac, iris all in high relief, are as smooth and mellow as ivory; the smallest rose or poppy on the tombs is an affair of twenty or thirty cornelians, onyxes, agates, jade, lapis lazuli, chrysolites. Special flower carvers from Bokhara were employed under a Hindu master craftsman for this *pieta dura* work. Though the minarets, so slender and tapering, are given some-what thick balconies and their white marble blocks are un-necessarily picked out with black edging, and though the elegant design of the whole Taj is limited to two contrasting forms, the onion dome and the flat rectangular wall, the total effect is to disarm most onlookers' criticism and, especially, by evening light, to involve them in its creator's melancholy-beautiful dream, whose splendour then seems to float like an opal-tinted cloud free of the earth.

Bullocks were pulling a lawnmower across the velvet turf as

we lingered in the gardens. One bullock lifted its tail, but before its dropping could reach the sward a small boy hopped out from behind a peepul tree and caught the steaming pat in a handful of grass. As Venus and Mercury came out in the lambent green-blue sky and the long shadows of the cypress became equally black, we looked back, from under Lord Curzon's lamp, half expecting the Taj's miracle to have vanished, an exquisite eastern illusion.

The next two days, in Uttar Pradesh and Bihar—at that time famine- and poverty-stricken states—were the hottest of the whole journey. We travelled through central north India from Agra to Muzaffarpur on the river Gandak, just above its junction with the Ganges. First we crossed the Jumna for Firozabad. Splashing every couple of hours at village wells and wetting shirts or wrapping wet towels round our heads to sit it out in the coach until the next 'cooler'—even swimming in a muddy backwater half-way—we made quite good going to Kanpur.

> The horrors of Cawnpore haunt me! Think of first the siege day and night, the crowds of helpless women and children with barely enough food, being kept for safety in the trenches with no pro-tection from the sun, and the agreement to march out (when the well dried up) if sent to Calcutta in boats. The Nana gave them the boats, then fired into them and sank them and massacred those who tried to land, and the remainder of the women and children he killed just as General Havelock came up. There must have been four or five hundred of them : 206 women and children were thrown into the well. (Lady Canning's Journal, 1857)

The ghat on the Ganges where this massacre took place long remained unaltered, even in the 'Manchester of India.'

We crossed over and came by early afternoon to Lucknow, whose dignified old colonial buildings and thronged streets sizzled under the zenith sun. (Iced lime juice or 'milk-rose' at the Kwality restaurant here gave us an air-conditioned break.) India has some of the finest examples of English architecture abroad : their sur-vivors give to Lucknow a special air and nostalgic appeal. The ruins of the Residency, used as a hospital during the siege, until its relief against odds of 7 to 1, are memorable—as are Edward

K

Lear's drawings of them. Left exactly as it was on the day when
the relieved garrison marched out, the Residency looks now like
an eighteenth-century Pompeii. The banqueting hall, which was
the hospital, is roofless and ivy-grown; plants sprout from the
fissures of the exposed brickwork. A colonnade shows bullet
marks in its battered plasterwork, while the scrollwork, surrounding the Wedgwood plaques on the elaborately stuccoed ceiling,
remains incongruously fresh. The pits of rubble have been turned
into a garden, with phlox and sweet peas, godetias and anti-
rrhinums on the borders of sweeping lawns, a poignant reminder
of the British love of flowers. The siege lasted from June to
October, the four hottest months here—when Lucknow's *shade*
temperature exceeds 117°F.

We continued in a heat daze by Bara to Faizabad and, as the
sun's brilliance began at last to dim, crossed the river Ghaghra
to Basti, a small town with one small-town type of hotel. We
slept out on its roof with mongoose for guardian, bare-bottomed
monkeys for company and mosquitoes for alarm clock. The cost :
½R each. A Sikh who had seen a newspaper photograph of the
coach came to greet us. An elderly Christian Indian came too to
bewail the sense of hopelessness and corruption in his State.

From Basti across the low-lying country to Gorakhpur it was
even hotter. This was a land of reed-thatched mud houses
clustered under date-palms and surrounded by brown baked clay,
where naked children, with the Hindu 'fate' cord round their
loins and thin 'pull to heaven' twist of hair on their scalps,
gathered listlessly to stare. A convoy of working elephants
dragged slowly along on the far side of the shade trees, the bullock carts had canopies to shield their driver from the sun; an
occasional palanquin type of rickshaw, with white embroidered
linen cloth on a bamboo frame, crowded with yellow-brown
faces, padded past. Purple convolvulus, Oxford-and-Cambridge
blue jays, scampering monkeys broke the monotony of the scene.

At one crossroads there was a village shrine, sugar-icing white,
with pink and blue images of Ganesh, the Hindu elephant god,
over the portico and a holy man streaked with gold paint and
shrouded in thin ropes of thigh-length hair.

We had hoped to cross our final river, the Gandak, at Pad-
rauna, so taking a reasonably direct route to the frontier. It was
not viable. We were out of Uttar Pradesh but Bihar had not
done with us yet. The set-back meant more sweltering hours,
driving south through surprised villages—almost tilting the thatch
off their close-set houses—in an outback area of unfinished 'direct
roads', often only hard-core wheel tracks, to reach a crossing
point. Back first to Kasia, then to Siwan, to Manjhi, to Chapra.
The sun sank, dusk quickly came, night closed in. At Chapra the
streets were impenetrable : a noisy wedding party with caparisoned white horses and white-glaring kerosene lamps blocked the
thoroughfare. We reached a dead-end and had to reverse; we
received unintelligible directions or vague assurances of 'good
bridge'. We avoided the direct road for Lalganj—the map sign
this time warned 'difficulties of passage'. Eventually, when nearly
at Patna, we made the crossing of the Gandak to Hajipur and
stopped in shabby crowded Muzaffarpur. We set bed-rolls down
at last inside the police station compound, avoiding the dried
excrement. Those who neglected to pull a sheet over their heads
gave the mosquitoes the best meal of their lives.

We were not sorry to leave Muzaffarpur—'Hustlefussabad'
Lear would have called it—and be out again among the mud
houses, the graceful leaning palms with their small feathery
heads, the occasional bright green banana plantation and groves
of dusty green mango trees or sugar cane that bordered the road
going north to Sagauli and Raxaul. Oxen were treading thin
crops in some of the baked iron-hard fields; in others small
bladder pods were being gathered. A glade and a pool before a
village shrine were rare delights in this parched land, which became barer and emptier of habitation the nearer we approached
the frontier to Nepal. At last, when the sun was at its most op-
pressive, and a hot wind blew through the open coach door, we
came into the dusty purlieus, the railway sidings and warehouses,
the shanty tea-houses and groaning bullock carts of Raxaul,
where a flimsy barrier stretches across the road to close off India.
We left the oven of the coach and made a rush for the tree-
shaded pump.

# 6 PARTS OF NEPAL

*The wildest dreams of Kew are the facts of Khatmandhu.*

Rudyard Kipling

The last leg of this new Grand Tour was a pioneer attempt by a British coach to reach the capital of Nepal. Frank now went ahead to Calcutta by train, to complete return trip arrangements. Bob was left as driver, courier, customs negotiator and master of our fate.

He seemed to be spending an inordinate time in the rickety upstairs office of the security post. True, it was siesta hour : men sprawled asleep under the arches of the Customs House shed; Sikh truckies played cards on the veranda of the tea-house; the black donkey-engine had ceased shunting goods wagons up and down on the narrow-gauge railway to Amlekhganj; Sherpa porters lounged in the shade; a heavy scent of frangipani blossom was wafted on the hot wind. Only the errands of a beautiful almond-eyed Nepalese girl, with shining black hair, red camellia set over an ear and a sinuous walk in her slender brown sari kept us from dozing off under the tree too. Eventually Bob called us over and we went up one at a time to confront a sleepy, slyly humorous officer, while he checked our documents and currency. The Nepalese government does not want to be saddled with 'hippies', any more than do the Afghan or Persian, and asks for confirmation of means before allowing some travellers in.

At last we got our visas checked, changed money and the barrier was lifted for us to proceed, 'For a single journey to the Kingdom of Nepal for visit to Kathmandu, Pokhara and Chitwan within a period of fifteen days from date of entry'. Per-

mission to tour outside Kathmandu valley must be obtained from
the foreign ministry. Until 1950 the whole country was practi-
cally inaccessible to people from the world outside : even after
Everest year, a royalty was exacted by the government from all
climbing expeditions, scaled according to height of peak. Everest
itself rated 3,000R.

This kingdom, whose treaty of friendship with Britain goes
back over one hundred years, made a friendly impression on us
from the outset. We welcomed the sight of hills, stretches of
timber, and wide stony river course after Bihar's stagnant flats.
We felt the atmosphere changing and smelt a whiff of clean
mountain air even across the twenty miles of banyans and swamp
of the Terai. We admired the terraced tillage and tiny, careful
rice fields, and as we came to Hitaura, the first chalet-style
buildings with their jutting eaves and carved struts out-thrust
from white walls. Many windows had intricately carved wooden
lattices. Sturdy, lighter-coloured, smiling people with a Mon-
golian look about eye and cheekbone, gave us welcome. Their
lively, playful grubby children swarmed about us. We found
two cheap hotels and split up between them. Wooden beds in
the gallery of rooms over the restaurant cost 2R; water supply
was short, but a bath in a tin bowl sufficed; the chicken, dahl and
rice were slow in appearing and smoked, the coffee indescribable,
but everybody smiled. Afterwards we shopped for the next day's
midday meal in the candlelit glow of open shops on a pitch-black
street. They sold tobacco, onions, small potatoes, cloth, lump salt
and various sorts of rice, but little else. Only the howling pariah
dogs seemed to resent our strangeness.

The coach left Hitaura on the Raj Path, the mountain highway linking Raxaul with Kathmandu, at six-thirty next day. By
then some of us were already on our way, savouring the fresh
morning air, the waking farms, the smiling country boys and girls
coming to school. Coolies gave us cheerful salutes as we walked up
to the first girder bridge in the river gorge. When we had been on
board again about half an hour an emergency sign confronted
us : ROAD BROKEN. Landslides and rockfalls had taken a section
of the Raj Path, carved out from the steep hill slopes, down with

them and no traffic could pass. Our eleven thousand mile journey looked like being halted within a hundred miles of its destination.

Bob had already reversed a short way when he noticed a heavy truck proceeding down the road ahead of us. It had not passed us nor we it and it apparently came from the north. A quick recce showed how : the river bed here was shallow and its shingly banks were crossed by wheel tracks. Obviously there was a river route feasible for a truck : it just might be possible for a coach. Nothing venture. . . . We investigated for sudden deep pools or boulder blocks. The river seemed fairly even both in depth and bed surface. So, by a smooth slope down the bank, Bob cautiously took to it. We crossed through shallows to use the gravel bank some half dozen times. Some of us went wading ahead thigh deep to clear awkward rocks, others to build up ramps to allow the coach to climb out of the water or to jack up the wheels on boulders when a sudden bump of ground was un-avoidable. Yard by yard Bob eased and swung and rocked the coach forward, and with the loss only of another section of side panel we at length drove out past the road break, found a slope to ascend from the river and were back again on the Raj Path.

The road now was a tourist's dream of the picturesque, a driver's hand-blistering nightmare with a coach of our size. There were constant twists and double bends of the tightest clearance, under the scraping threat of cliffs and massive boulders and one particularly spectacular crag known as the 'lover's chair'. We were carried high above impenetrable gorges, with forest folded endlessly into forest over rock that had the savagery of iron con-torted by the sun. Down the precipitous slopes hung great gnarled trees of white and deep red rhododendron, while yellow roses of Sharon, tiny white Himalayan roses, scarlet poinsettia and bril-liant blue Alpines clothed the sides of every ravine.

At the first feasible side valley Bob pulled up. Lunch, not in the sulphurous dust of Indian roads, but within reach of a spark-ling stream under a tonic sun, with inspiring terrain and in-vigorating air. In the thicket of thorns beyond the grassy slope fluttered swallowtail butterflies, a bizarre variety barred brown and white in horizontal stripes, and a pair of magnificent, large

velvety black and delphinium blue that hovered like humming-
birds. Brilliant dragonflies quartered the stream, wild strawberries
covered the banks and, in this horticulturalist's paradise, there
were blue primula, geranium, azalea, white magnolia, white
cornus, camellia and the single chrysanthemum. Pine, deodar,
spruce and fir contested every yard of soil and light in the forest
surrounds, which harbour deer and antelope. Actually all that
we saw on legs was a walnut-wrinkled barefoot woman, with
large brass earrings, brass studs round the edge of her ears and
a brass ring in one nostril. She appeared from nowhere carrying
a big, loaded straw skip on her back, supported by a braided
band round her forehead, and came timidly up to see if we intended leaving behind any useful jars or tins.

The climb continued, with Bob twisting and heaving at the
wheel, up a spur of the Mahabharat Range, round the endless
hairpins until we came out to the Horticultural Research Station
of Daman, at about 8,000ft and some fifty miles from Kathmandu. A modern tower with observation gallery stands close by
the road, and at the right time and season offers a view of the
Himalayas 'in one glittering arc from Dhaulagiri and Annapurna
to Sagarmatha (Mount Everest).' We ascended, took tea, but had
no view : sunrise is the best bet. Another time, perhaps.

We wound down now in a spectacular descent from Daman to
Palung, Tistung and Thankot. Forest, rock and scrub gave place
to the first high slopes of cultivation, rising in terraces like the
irregular steps of pyramids up the foothills. Among the vivid
green fields neat, two-storeyed brick and plaster houses, some
painted warm yellow or blood red, and thatched with reeds,
gave the landscape a familiar *Geographical Magazine* look.
Women and children crowded at doorways, women of smooth
handsome face, with long dark plaits intertwined with red
wool, and in bright red or gentian blue bodice, long skirt and
broad waistband. Many carried a child on back or hip by a long
scarf. All smiled and waved. On this exhilarating road, weaving
up and round the foothills, we came finally to a police checkpoint
in a straggling village. Then we were out into the green oval of
the wide valley and the grove of trees beside the sacred Bagmati

river that herald Kathmandu, a scene with the antique delicacy of a willow-pattern plate.

In a small dusty square, not far from the new GPO Bob pulled on the brakes with blistered hands and decanted us towards the Panorama Hotel. We had made it. For half a dozen of us this completed the journey, begun in February, ended in May. The rest would travel forward by coach to Calcutta, for Bangkok, Darwin, Perth, Melbourne, Sydney, Wagga-Wagga or Tokyo.

Kathmandu is a living legend. Its valley surrounded by tier upon tier of green hills overtopped by snow-clad peaks blooms with pagodas, shrines and temples. Its people are hardy, independent, friendly and colourful. Their culture, which blends Buddhism with Hinduism, is not of the museum order, but in daily evidence. Whilst in the Hindu pantheon Gautama Buddha appears sometimes as a reincarnation of Krishna, the Buddhist of Kathmandu can see Krishna in lotus posture at the side of Gautama himself. No people could observe more frequent or more spectacular festivals. For the folk-lorist and photographer, the trekker and Tantric art enthusiast, the naturalist and seeker after nirvana opportunities of all kinds abound. One needs only a day or two to recognise that here, in one valley, are the heaped up rewards of all Grand Tours and the fallacy of the saying that it is better to travel hopefully than to arrive.

After a final meal in coach company at the Panorama Hotel, we who were staying on transferred our baggage elsewhere. All types of accommodation can be found in Kathmandu, from the first class 'Annapurna' or the climbers' inimitable 'Royal'—where marijuana grows wild in the surrounding fields and Coca-Cola is prohibited—to recent compromises with the Peace Corps generation such as the 'Camp' hotel, or in various outlying bungalows and hostels. We found rooms, bare, but cool and clean, with a tap and tea-roses in the courtyard, run by a courteous Buddhist and his watchful son, for 5R; a bed in the common sleeping room was 3R. There was a place to eat just opposite with Tibetan cook, Tashi, and two brisk boy waiters, Karma and Angtak : boiled veg and buff steak were the staple menu.

In many parts Kathmandu represents what medieval Europe once was: narrow jostling thoroughfares of open stalls; dark, wooden houses and murderous alleys; stench, ordure, flies; grotesque images and elaborate shrines; priests, porters, beggars, animals; artistic treasures and mumbo-jumbo; abject squalor and brilliant costumes, all cheek by jowl.

As we saw the coach party off at 6 am next day men were bathing and washing their clothes at a sunken tank with lion head spouts surmounted by gilded statues of Ganesh. Women performed *their* toilet over the gutter outside their black, cave-like rooms in the old wooden houses and 'bottomed' their babies, 'nitted' their children's heads or suckled their newest infant while having their hair combed and dressed with ribbon. Dogs nosed in the surrounding refuse and excrement. Peons in flowered caps staggered past under yokes and double baskets of vegetables, bales of straw, baulks of timber or loads of bricks; further down the street, round the courtyard of Asan Annapurna temple families of squatters peered out of galleried recesses at us and their sprawling children. On the crumbling gate the figures of Vishnu and his consort Parvati are entwined, priapic stone gods fill the wall niches, the massive image of a sacred ox glares stonily down and an elaborate pinnacle crowned with four brass cobras stands in the middle. Eaves, lintels and embrasures of this neglected idolaters' fantasy run riot in intricate wood-carving.

We came through Juddha Sadak— a street developed 'to meet modern requirements', now the main hub of the city, as it might equally be of, say, Patna or Jammu—past the open market and, rounding a corner, we confronted the remarkable Durbar Square. Only small—though with many streets and bazaar lanes radiating from it—it proffered a medley of Oriental architecture stranger and more powerful than that in any other city yet visited.

As the residential area of the rulers of Nepal this square, Hanuman Dhoka, epitomises the old religious and cultural life. It contains the Taleju (1549) temple dedicated to Tulaja Devi, protectress of the Maharaja's house; the 40ft figure in red, black and orange masonry of Kal Bhairab, God of Destruction; the

gilded portals to the palace with their great griffin guardians and
ever watching Buddha's eyes; the pagoda of the Basantpur
Durbar rising in dark carved wooden galleries to nine storeys;
the statue of Raja Pratap Malla and his four sons on a
column with cobra and lotus capital; the Big Bell, the Big Drum,
the shrouded figure of the Monkey God, under its golden umbrella, guarding the seat of royalty, and various other pagoda-
style temples. This plunge into an alien cultural world was almost
too sharp for belief. These exotic forms could not, surely, be part
of the everyday texture of a 'Scooteaway' taxicab city? But a
passing patrol of mounted Gurkhas and the removal into custody
of a Newar woman, with hands tied and crossed over her bare
breasts, indicated the realities.

Seen at close quarters, Kala Bhairab, the fearsome idol gazing
out at street level, clutching *her* breasts with two hands, waving
a spear and firebrand with two others and trampling on the head
of a demon, jerked reality out of focus again. Her forehead was
strung with a row of skulls, great pendants of them encircled her
neck and monstrous paunch, while smears of ghee, vermilion
powder and a scatter of marigold heads spoke of her continued
măna. The Tantric temple close by, carved from pediment to
roof and coloured in bright greens, blues, reds and yellows
showed up other extraordinary dream images. Horned ibex
totems with large erect phalluses acted as roof supports at each
corner among smiling multi-armed female caryatids : by way of
frieze, the acts describable in a less inhibited Kama Sutra were
executed in lively bas-relief as public blueprints for gymnastic
coupling. A smiling simplicity about this paean to procreation
and love-making in broad day contrasted favourably with the
obscurantism of the Ganesh image in a nearby shrine. Hidden
behind a link scree and shrouded in green and pink muslin, in
the dense smoke of incense and votive oil lamps black with
grease, it was constantly visited by women with offerings of rice,
coins or flowers. The children made fun of both—playfully ringing Ganesh's heavy prayer bell as they passed and pelting each
other with stones under the Tantric couplings.

In the thronged streets of overhanging wooden houses, over-

flowing shop-fronts and overpowering smells that form the old
bazaar, we found the human mixture more various even than in
Chandni Chouk or Meshed circus. Bespectacled, shaven-headed
Buddhist monks with saffron robes and raised black umbrellas
walked through, oblivious of all comers; Sherpa porters staggered
under their incredible loads; a rickshaw boy with a consignment
of black pigs tied on pushed a way in; long-gowned and girdled
Tibetan women went quietly about their shopping; Newar
women—from the tribes regarded as the earliest inhabitants of
Nepal, later subjugated by the Gurkhas—chattered in their
finery of black or purple velvet bodices, bright blue, deep red,
yellow or viridian green flowered skirts and white waistbands.
Red flowers were in their hair, crimson-dye in the partings,
jewelled stars or rings in their ears, gold spots on their foreheads
and clashing silver-gilt bracelets on wrist and ankle. A woman
with a three-year-old child at the swollen nipple of a dirty breast
offered cream-and-black patterned blankets for sale; exquisite
slender girls in pale lilac, jade or lime-green saris were followed
by the glazed eyes of stick-thin beggars; weather-beaten women
with heavy slung loads jostled roughly past; country girls spread
wild strawberries and yellow mountain raspberries out on large
leaves at 25p each; parrots perched before shops in which everything from a cobra-designed bronze oil cruse to a plastic Japanese
thermos flask hung from serried hooks. Boys offering to change
'big notes' for fancy amounts hung about alley entrances;
bicyclists rang frantically for passageway, naked children chew-
ing betel or sugar cane, clutched at one for 'paisa, pice'; tall,
pink Peace Corps workers sauntered through and slant-eyed
Chinese shopkeepers met their curious requests with smiles. The
bazaar's friendliness was scarcely less than its bustle : we were
absorbed into the amiable, picturesque unselfconscious squalor
of Nepal.

As we passed the lion portals of the Temple of the Living
Goddess, Kumari Devi, from the carved wooden balcony on
which a child of twelve in red robe, hair top-knot and heavy
kohl, appears as the Goddess's living representative at the temple
guardian's nod, and into the lane leading to the river, a pro-

cession approached. Men in white or grey head-shawls, preceded by drums and cymbals, carried a figure on a bier wrapped in white cerecloth and reed matting, the whole covered by a red and orange pall. A young man behind ululated loudly among a crowd of sympathisers : his attendants scattered rice and millet over the doorsteps. They skirted a filthy dung yard where a partly dismembered bullock lay in its orange-yellow skin, while crows, dogs and flies swarmed round its severed head. Women were waiting at the river and wailed loudly as porters carried over bundles of straw through the shallows. The whole procession followed; the mourners ritually washed their hands and feet : the body was laid on a concrete square. The young man— the dead's eldest son—now wrapped himself in a white sheet and intoned with a priest as he walked round the body sprinkling ghee, flowers and rice.

A pyre was made with wood and straw on a raised brick incinerator; when it was complete the old man's body, stripped of cerecloth and matting, was laid on top in his ordinary cotton clothes, more bundles of straw were placed over him and a flame applied. There were loudly renewed wails until the wood caught and a thin smoke spiralled up against the sun to the trees where vultures sat. Four hours afterwards as we came back to the ghat two or three old men were still poking about for bones in the pile of ashes.

Upstream buffaloes were bathing and a country lane led by an avenue of bottle-brush trees to a row of galleried wooden houses, where women sat spinning wool or weaving ornamental carrying slings like the Aran Island 'crios'. After a mile we came to the steps at the hill-foot of Swayambunath Temple. The steps, some five hundred of them, climbed through tangled woods infested with monkeys, in mounting steepness to a broad site 250ft above the valley base. At the foot sit twin Buddhas in the lotus position : they are four or five times human size and painted bright yellow for the flesh, scarlet for the robes and blue on eyelids, eyebrows and curled hair. A score of niches in their canopies once held Bodhisattvas, but all but a few have been taken. The head of this long, static escalator is alive with dragons, horses,

elephants in stone—and real monkeys swinging down from the
overhanging trees. To peel a banana is to ask for trouble—
especially from one of the females with a baby clinging on
underneath.

On mounting the final high steps one confronts architectural
bedlam. The main structure, the chaitya, is a solid hemisphere
of brick and earth painted white, supporting a conical spire in
gleaming copper gilt from whose four-sided base the all-seeing
blue, black and white eyes of Buddha stare hypnotically. The
spire can be seen for many miles around, and the site of stupa
and Buddhist temple adjoining is over two thousand years old.
Round the hemisphere of the chaitya worn Tibetan prayer wheels
are constantly rotated by devotees. In the courtyard are other
temples of Hindu gods, a statue of the Thunderbolt God of Ram
and a whole series of miniature stupas over which the monkeys
lollop. A priest sits on the ground murmuring incantations before
little clay pots of rice, wicks burning in ghee, sweet peas and
flower petals, while women crowd round with their offerings.
Some musicians squat in a tight circle to make pandemonium
with drums, cymbals and long, slender horns. Three handsome
Nepalese girls stand by dressing each other's hair. A man comes
to feed the monkeys with pieces of paw-paw. The great bell
rings and in the temple, which houses a huge, age-blackened
figure of Buddha, acolytes with shaven heads and saffron robes
put renewed vigour into their endless chanting of prayers. At
the back squat a few mat-haired hippies amid the grime and
grease and pall of incense. The precincts mask their sanctity
under indescribable dirt, animal and vegetable refuse.

From Swayambunath a fenced path led through barley fields
and thickets of bamboo, with honeysuckle and wild rose, cuckoos
and Indian robins, past a site for a modern industrial and re-
frigeration plant, to the Balaju Water Gardens. Balaju is Kathmandu's Shalimar, with a difference. There are brilliant flower-
beds, exotic grafted orchids, magnificent Scots pine on the hill
slopes, large orange and black and white butterflies, an image of
Sleeping Vishnu—but instead of the iridescent parade of saris on
fragile, sallow-dark figures, here a gaggle of laughing schoolgirls

is going for swimming instruction to the Olympic-size baths. In the garden young men scrub themselves before sluicing under one of the twenty-two spouting dragon-heads of the open tank.

Bicycles are popular in Nepal. We hired some and rode out to Chobar Gorge through which all the river water has its outlet. Tradition says this gorge was cut by the god Manjusri to drain the whole valley, then a lake. In the roadside fields women were digging in teams with short-handled spades. Among the hamlets of painted, straw-roofed houses, they were grinding corn in a small hole in the earth with wooden pestles used see-saw fashion. The hill above the gorge has a picturesque temple of Adinath and offers an excellent panorama of the whole sinuous terraced countryside.

Another ride took us out of the capital by New Road Gate to Patan. We passed a temple with four rampant griffins and a splendid pillar statue, crossed the river and then cruised along frangipani scented roads to the rough cobbled entry of the 'City of Beauty'. Lalitpur or Lalitapatan is celebrated for its fine arts, to which a new industrial estate has recently added metal furniture, carpets, nails, screens and batteries.

First impression was of deserted courtyards, noisome pot-holed alleys and a sombre Durbar Square. Patan, stormed in the seventeenth century by the Raja Pratap Malla, the same whose statue adorns Kathmandu square, was sacked and desecrated a century later, during the Gurkha conquest, by Prithvi Narayan and still breathes an air of remembered defeat. There are many mutilated sculptures, stone idols split apart, collapsed gates and temples with their finial umbrellas snarled into rusted iron. What remains of its former glories, however, is peculiarly impressive.

The ornately carved three-tier stone temple, for example, built in 1630 to Lord Krishna in Durbar Square, is decorated with war scenes from Hindu epics. Around it there are memorial pillars to kings and generals or winged gods, while pagoda roofs with erotically carved and coloured struts, rise on all sides in diminishing piles. The courtyard of Kerabahal has another three-tier pagoda style temple, golden this time in honour of Buddha. Its priests and acolytes sit there reading from their wooden-leaved texts. More shrines and temples occur round every corner. A side street contains one with a really massive prayer-wheel : another, Mahabandha, has Buddha figures on each terra-cotta brick. At the cardinal points of Patan, just outside the city, there are four ancient stupas, or mound temples, said to have been erected by the Emperor Asoka of India, when he came north on Buddhist pilgrimage in the third century BC. He also visited Swayam-bunath.

Streets and lanes radiate in all directions from Durbar Square through lesser squares and tols, where the Indian and Tibetan traders set out their wares and where the famous Patan craft-work vies with the work of the newer cottage industries. As the Newars of old enriched temples and houses with wood-carving at its most sumptuous and elaborate, so Nepalese craftsmen now produce elaborately embossed and chased silverware, fearsome papiermâché masks, turquoise inset snuff-boxes and finger rings, articles of buffalo horn and gilded copper as well as traditional statuettes and fine rugs of soft wool. 'Tankas' could be bought here at from 2,000R for an exquisite five hundred year old specimen embroidered in silk on velvet, down to 150R for the painted-on-cloth type of a century old. Their prayer on the reverse read, in Tibetan, 'Good luck, health and happiness to all descendants'.

By late-afternoon Durbar Square livened up. Stalls opened round Krishnu Mandir : a white-suited old man under a large black umbrella went the rounds with a white-smocked coolie to carry for him; bent double, simian-faced women peered from under their head-slings and heavy loads; young porters trotted by with round baskets on swinging yokes; barefooted women in long red or green skirts, bound with a cummerbund used as purse, shopped for onions, red peppers, cauliflowers, radishes, tiny tomatoes and melon; naked, dusty infants called 'Hallo', 'Bye-bye'. At a sunken tank an athletic brown saddhu briskly stripped to his G-string, soaped thoroughly, washed and then did gymnastic exercises—without upsetting his long black hair or spoiling the gold stripes on his brow. Groups in the colourful Newar costume, with sarong skirts and silver-gilt ear and nose ornaments, were coming in from the country. In a courtyard we found a tea-house with a sunken shrine inlaid with flowered tiles and shielded by four brass pythons holding a canopy, from which to view the passing show. When we emerged the sky behind the looming tiers of the pagoda temples was inflamed by a thundery orange-yellow sunset that glinted theatrically on the assemblage of pillars, pinnacles, stupas and elephant gods.

Patan should be seen during one of the spectacular festivals—Machendranath Rath Jatra, the chariot festival (whose vehicle was laid up near the huge prayer wheel), held for a week during April; or during Tihnar, the festival of lights held in October. The first two days of Tihnar are dedicated to the crow and the dog, the third and fifth to Laxmi, goddess of plenty; then lamps are set at night in all the windows of houses and shops so that the whole city sparkles with light.

Kathmandu is the magnet for all sorts of 'seekers'. Our lodging housed two Austrians come to do the thirty-two day Everest trek to Namche Bazaar and Thyangboche : a Japanese student hoping to find work as a fisherman in Iceland; a middle-aged American hooked on the trail of 'hippydom' and psychedelic art; a Canadian returning by local bus and truck from the Australian outback via Afghanistan; a Kensington 'flower child', picking over Nepalese designs for fabric patterns; a restless round-the-worlder, anxious to be photographed with his 'jumbo' pack, en route for Ceylon; a handsome Dutch girl travelling on her own and just back from Pokhara; pilgrims to Lumbini's old monastery and the reputed birthplace of Gautama Buddha; and of course Peace Corps vacationists. Whatever else they were after, nearly all wanted a glimpse of Annapurna or Machapuchare or, if possible, Everest.

The road to the town of Bhadgaon crosses the wide, sacred river, winds uphill through a straggle of wood-carved houses, past barley and vegetable fields, their hedges pink with wild roses, beyond the modern, multi-purpose school built with American aid, then up to the Gurkha infantry barracks and parade ground. It was here that the loads were dumped and sorted for

the successful British Everest expedition of 1953. Squads of cheerful, stocky, darkly sunburned recruits, in their starched bottle-
green, were being drilled at the double on the parched grass:
their corporal grinned a greeting. 'From here', says the local
guide, 'on clean days one can have fine views of snowy ranges.'

Bhadgaon, 'city of devotees' was founded nearly six hundred
years later than Patan by Raja Ananda Malla and developed in
the shape of the conch shell of Vishnu Narayan. As we came in
by the old cobbled way the traditional industries, pottery and
weaving, were in evidence. Down every alley posts and trestles
supported skeins of yarn a hundred feet long; women in pairs
walked the length of them with their twisting distaffs to make
the weft for rugs and carpets. Colours were arranged so as to
make borders of red, black or blue; when complete the frames
could be turned through 90° for the warp process. The streets
became wider and cleaner, the buildings better—unlike Patan,
Bhadgaon had surrendered without resistance to Prithvi Narayan
—and we came from the half shadow of houses into an arena
of shimmering gold.

When our eyes adjusted to a scene containing over a dozen
Buddhist and Hindu style buildings in blinding sun we could
scarcely tear them away from the dominating piece of architecture, the five-storeyed Nyatapola Temple, most handsome
pagoda in Nepal. The great flight of entrance steps is flanked by
gigantic figures. Two heavily moustached strongmen at the foot,
then two elephants, two lions, two griffins and on the top step
the 'terrible deities' Singhini and Baghini, the tiger and lion.
Each pair of figures is considered ten times as strong as the pair
below, and the two strongmen, Jaya Malla and Phatta, ten times
as strong as any human. Erected in Raja Bhupatindra Malla's
time, 1708, 'with the help of the gods', the temple's tradition is
that the gods' subsequent revels were so flagrant and debauched
that even Tantric worshippers were frightened off. So it remains
untenanted. One wonders what these revels could have involved
after looking more attentively at Pashupatinath temple, 'noted
for its wood carving and erotic pictures'. The frieze of this contains a score of 'positions' involving two, three or four men and

L

women and animals. King Malla, however, has a fine gold-plated statue, seated in the act of worship, on the lotus capital of a monolith.

There is also the huge bronze curfew bell, mounted on a 20ft cube of stone and rung every morning when the Goddess Taleju is worshipped; a lesser bronze bell, known as the Bell of Barking Dogs—its sound said to be a replica of the sound of Death—was hung by the Raja to scare away devils. His statue looks across at the finest building of his reign, the durbar hall whose dazzling golden gate is forbidden to photographers. Intricately embossed with monsters both Buddhist and Hindu, dragons, lizards, lions, elephants, mermen, scrolls, bells and leaves with over all the multi-armed figure of Kali riding on a Garuda, this 'most lovely piece of art in the whole kingdom' flashes like a many-faceted jewel in its handsome setting. Even more remarkable perhaps is the wood-carved masterpiece of the Palace of Fifty-five Windows, and the peacock-in-full-pride carved on the window lattice of an old monastery, in one of the residential streets.

After such a surfeit of sun on gold one may pass the Lion Gate and its seventeenth-century stone figures of Hanuman, Bhairab and Narsingha Narayan, to enter the picture gallery. There are treasures of astonishing richness here too : scroll and book illustrations from various schools of Tantric art, pictures of cabalistic meaning made up of masonic signs, pictures in Sino-Japanese style, allegorical Indian pictures of Ganesh, Kali and the Trinity : Brahma the Creator, Vishnu the Preserver, Siva the Destroyer and Reproducer. There are exquisitely ornate and ancient tankas and cunning variants, barely detectable in their embraces, of the god-in-copulation theme. A discreet, patient attendant led us through its low arches into the complex sequence of rooms : for what they held alone it was worth coming to Nepal.

Bhadgaon is indeed the Golden City : people in the streets seem under its spell. Sleepy old men selling vegetables sit cross-legged beneath oiled paper parasols painted with dragons; flag-like lengths of black and red block-printed material hang outside the red painted shops : creamy-brown women wash themselves to the navel, delightfully unabashed, in the public fountains;

spinners and weavers trace their leisurely patterns in the alleys; smiling children show the way to yet another tank or temple— perhaps that made from the trunk of a single tree. The sun beats down, carved into kaleidoscopic patterns on the flagstones by balcony grilles; the gold images flash and sparkle with their own esoteric life; a Tibetan shepherd brings his herd of goats to rest in the square near a pile of hubble-bubble vessels by the potters. 'Namuste' they greet us raising palm-joined hands.

Few could leave Kathmandu and turn their backs on Everest without giving it at least a second chance to reveal itself. Thyang- boche or even Kakani being too far out of our way, we chose Nagarkot, only ten miles from Bhadgaon, as the possible view- point. We walked there in an afternoon from the Gurkha parade ground, across sweltering paddy fields, past toy-like hamlets on remote terraced slopes of rice and rye, up rough, bouldery, heat- cracked slopes bright with clumps of cotoneaster, poinsettia and great green blisters of cactus, to a stone-built bungalow, Mount Everest Lodge. It was near the highest point of the ridge and offered 'food and lodging for tourists and travellers on the top of a high mountain.' We were given Chinese blankets, a hurricane lantern, tots of rakai and promise of a call for rising before dawn.

We rose before light. A cool mist clung to us in pearly droplets. We reached the ridge crest high above the snow-fed Indravati river—the crest from which 'sunrise and sunset over Everest and other snow peaks are breath-taking.' We waited : light gradually infiltrated the grey shadows. We moved along to a better vantage point. Light increased and we could discern faintly a great valley full of dense pockets of mist; then endless green terraced slopes falling away to unseen depths. Beyond, a vast anvil-shaped cloud and towering cumulus shrouded the major peaks of all the Nepalese Himalayas. We waited another hour. Light improved to morning brightness—but the sun, and Sagarmatha, stayed re- mote, invisible . . . another time?

# 7 WAYS AND MEANS

For a tour of the kind sketched here there can be no hard and fast lines. Flexibility, improvisation and hunch all play their part. But for travellers setting out for the first time there are some considerations to heed and some doubts to remove.

How to go and with whom? The question of how depends chiefly on the time and means at disposal, the kind of comfort and company desired. If you define yourself as young, tough and keen to travel far, cheaply and fairly rough, the Personal Column advertisements in the Sunday newspapers will introduce you to like-minded travellers with trips planned, either on a commercial or social basis. Some offer Kathmandu by mini-bus for under £70, some a crossing of the Great Salt Desert to southern Persia or trip to the nomad ground of the Hindu Kush by Land-Rover; one promises Kabul and back, the return by covered truck, for £25 in time for students' university term in October. The accent here is likely to be on informality of organisation, smaller groups, and helping with maintenance and the chores.

If you want the excitement of an adventurous journey without too much cutting of comfort or cost, in the last ten years a variety of companies have established themselves whose advertisements in the newspapers' travel sections speak for themselves. The average age of their passengers tends to rise in ratio to the appeal of air-conditioned, custom-built coaches, pre-booked hotel accommodation and courier service; larger numbers on regular schedules will help to keep costs down and competition to keep standards up. Some tour operators specifically 'do not camp or tow a sleeping compartment', although they do give choice between sharing rooms and 'superior accommodation'.

Those whose sights are set between these two modes, the cheapest happy-go-lucky and the moderately luxurious, will also find scope. More than one operator has seen the virtue of combining conveyance, guidance and advice with considerable latitude for passengers to work things out as best for themselves—a mixture adopted by the Sundowners which the writer found to his taste. All, of course, except the 'Have-jeep-need-passenger(s)-share-funds' type, will normally keep within an advertised route and time allowance. The glossier the brochure, probably the less elastic the routine.

With whom to go? It is easier to say, both on personal and communal grounds, with whom not to go. Individuals and groups brought close together every day for two or three months in new, inescapable and sometimes fairly trying conditions, need mutual tolerance, warmth and humour to get the best out of the journey. One persistent grouser can spoil a whole party; anyone with an overdose of starch or ginger in their make-up is a doubtful travelling companion. But extremes may meet happily.

When to go and with what preparation? Favoured time for departure from England to the East is September, so that climatic conditions in India can be best on arrival. As alternative mid-February departure means leaving the slush of winter behind and enjoying a succession of spring seasons warmer than in England, so gradually acclimatising to Indian weather. By the time the temperature tops 90°F one can generally put up with it, even enjoy it. Certain companies perhaps panic unnecessarily about avoiding deep freeze and hot weather travel; some temperaments thrive on it.

Preparations are of two sorts, necessary and anticipatory. It is *necessary* to have a passport valid for and with enough page space for the duration of the journey; an International Certificate of Vaccination with current inoculation stamps for smallpox and cholera (the combined cholera/TAB vaccination is recommended to cover also typhoid and paratyphoid); visas for certain countries. Commonwealth citizens need visas for Iran, Afghanistan and, when tours include it, Iraq. Non-Commonwealth citizens need them for Pakistan and India also. These should be obtained before departure, and a spare half-dozen passport type photographs should be taken for forms en route. A personal travel insurance for the period of the journey, covering life, medical expenses and loss of baggage is generally stipulated by the operator if not covered under the terms of the tour.

Anticipatory preparations can to some extent be modified by an individual according to his experience. Health is important for enjoyment; neglected, it costs much to restore once abroad. So to have it and one's teeth in order before departure is a matter of prudence. Preventatives—paludrine for malaria (a few doses before entering Turkey), palliatives for diarrhoea, salt tablets for heat exhaustion, mylol for insects—are small things to carry and tried safeguards. Aspirin and an antiseptic may have their uses, as also, for many, will sunglasses and a headscarf or sun hat, if only against dust. Water-purifying tablets will counteract its local risks, in lieu of the bottled or mineral sort.

Money, luggage and food all need forethought. The safe way to carry money is in traveller's cheques, the safe place (for cash) in a body belt, 'digger' fashion, or in a small linen bag hung round one's neck. Cash often obtains a better rate of exchange, though at times it does not do as well. To take both cheques and cash, some in smaller units, gives one chance to break even and also to avoid piling up foreign currency surplus as result of cashing a cheque when almost due to cross a frontier. Two notecases, or billfolds, can also be useful: one for the current spending money of the country, the other for the reserve, separately stowed. When the writer had his pocket picked it was the former that went, a lesser evil! Camping travellers get by on a daily budget of ten shillings or even less, modest hotel users need from twenty to twenty-five shillings as an average over the whole trip, those wanting something better thirty-five.

Luggage is usually restricted in weight and/or size of container, for ease of handling and reasonable loading of the vehicles; it does *not* demand best leather bags. The strong, medium-sized fabric suitcase, the zip-up canvas grip or overnight bag may not come through unscathed, but at least their wear and tear will be more bearable. Between forty and fifty pounds

for the weight of case and bag combined is the normal limit.
Most tour operators fight shy of metal-framed rucksacks, as
awkward in shape and destructive in contact when stowing luggage. Most, again, make an extra weight allowance for passengers' sleeping-bags and air mattresses, if camping features:
they can be expected to provide the tentage and stoves, kettles
and pans, while individuals bring their own cup, plate(s) and
cutlery. Some companies provide camp beds and double (thick)
sleeping-bags, suitable even for sub-zero camping, as well. Carrying firearms is usually forbidden.

Foreign food surprises, delights, bores or, at times, sets up
antipathies. In Greece and Turkey one follows their good habit
of seeing it in the restaurant kitchen first. On desert runs it may
be scarce. Trips of the safari type with estate cars in convoy allow
up to fifteen-pound food parcels. For others the half a dozen tins
for emergency use are left to passengers' discretion. Apart from
this one can restore a flagging appetite, vary a surfeit of rice or
dahl, eke out a thin diet with a few familiar, tasty items such as
sardines, meat paste, honey or marmalade, bacon, coffee, sweet-
ened milk, packet soup, without making too big a hole in the
weight allowance or a possible mess by including them in the
luggage. A large Thermos for iced drinks and a small Primus and
pan are an asset: Primus fuel is obtainable almost everywhere.
And one can replenish stocks, sometimes even with the same
brand of goods, at several unusual grocers—in Hamadan, Isfahan, Meshed, Kandahar. Otherwise local marketing is half the
fun: and for most buying or selling English plus a bit of German
will usually be sufficient. Salads and any peeled fruit are sources
of risk to avoid in cholera areas.

The considerations for clothing are comfort, coolness and extra
warmth; and as little weight as possible. Casual styles, drip-dry
for ease of washing, 'peel-off' woollens, wind-cheaters, jeans and
perhaps an all-purpose dufflecoat, are the thing; a pair of lined
boots as well as sandals; T-shirts or cotton dresses as well as heavy
sweaters; 'smalls' both temperate and tropical. Variations in
temperature with February departures are considerable. Hot
weather countries usually have good laundry facilities, so that

changes can be made often without too many duplicated garments. A better dress, shirt, slacks, jacket, for an occasion, is also
a morale booster. Very few pack too little; nearly all find they
could have done with less. The extra space, after adding spare
toilet items of one's regular choice—they will be neither as cheap
nor as easy to find abroad—takes care of the traveller's ac-
quisitions. 'Esso' filling stations, it is worth noting, provide clean
wash-rooms en route.

For those who wish to receive periodical mail from home, tour
operators usually arrange to call at American Express, British
Embassy or Cook's offices at a few points for its collection and
indicate the latest posting date for its timely arrival. It is also
possible, but expensive, to post home in the ordinary way un-
wanted clothing.

The camera user also needs to anticipate conditions. Film,
especially colour, besides being harder to find and possibly less
reliable, is also more expensive in eastern countries. Supplies for
the journey should be bought before departure : the customs
allow through quite generous amounts for personal use. In prolonged heat exposed film may deteriorate : for safety it should be
despatched for processing instead of being carried home. The
writer found a separate camera for colour and for black-and-
white an advantage and in some respects an economy.

Photography is not welcomed everywhere, a fact easy to forget
in the excitement of the moment. Subjects in military or famine
areas, at border posts and bridges and dams, in mosques or
among Moslems, especially women, are obvious risks. It is best
to avoid any likelihood of offence to security or to local suscepti-
bility. One has seen cameras stripped of film and heard of them
smashed by those offended.

Strong traditions and religious beliefs carry over into daily
affairs, including food, drink and dress. Turks, for instance, are
sensitive about the fez and the veil, now that they are out. The
strict Moslem does not eat pork or take spirits, but eats beef and
smokes; he shaves his head, washes hands and feet before prayer,
holds Sabbath on Friday and buries the dead. The Sikh eats
pork and drinks spirits, but does not smoke; he grows his hair

long and always covers it. The Hindu never eats meat—or willingly eats with those who do; he baths daily, holds Sabbath on Tuesday and burns the dead. In some Indian states there is prohibition and an official liquor permit is required for tourist purchase of wine, beer or spirits. In Moslem countries a women's uncovered arms, shoulders or legs cause offence—as do slacks when tight. To enter a Moslem or Hindu temple shoes must be removed, and in Hindu temples all leatherware is prohibited.

Religious festival dates and monsoon dates may also, if ignored, hinder progress. In India rice harvest in October or November is followed by light rain in January; wheat harvest in spring by 'mango showers' (freak storms) in May; the heavy monsoon rains come in mid-June and last into September. Ramadan and No-Ruz, Holi and Muharram, among other fast days, festivals and anniversaries, change the pattern of work in Hindu or Moslem communities. To find out their times beforehand will obviate relying on a shop, office, garage or even part of a town being open, when it may be closed or closed off for a day or days.

Journeying into unknown parts without some sort of guide is not unlike going in blinkers. It may produce pleasant surprises but can cause whole prospects to be missed. On the other hand no one wants to be nose-led every step, even on a journey 'into the history of man' such as this. Background information, lively, up-to-date and succinct, in a form handy and cheap for the pocket, is provided by the series of Vista Books. They cover the historical, social and artistic ground in most of the countries here traversed and add just enough practical information for either reading beforehand or grasping on the journey. At frontiers free brochures on individual cities and special regions, with folding plans, can usually be obtained. The real enthusiast will find in *Centres of Art and Civilisation* (Elek Books) eight or nine of the great cities of Europe, the Middle East and India treated with the opulence of colour and black-and-white illustration that their art and architecture deserve. For the rest a party on tour generally has its well-thumbed books, if only for relaxation.

Over the European section of the New Grand Tour operators vary their routes. The writer has reached Venice via the French

and Italian Rivieras and also by way of Heidelburg, Munich,
Salzburg and the Brenner; others prefer Vienna to Venice, proceeding thence to Belgrade and Sofia for Istanbul. Which way to
take? Only the individual can decide how strong for him is the
pull of the Mediterranean. In normal peaceful times the alternative route offered from Istanbul to Tehran is by Ankara, Beirut,
Jerusalem, Amman and Baghdad in place of the south coast (or
Black Sea coast) and highlands of Turkey. What is the best
choice? Again not even the traveller who has done both can
decide. So much depends on what one finds and what one seeks.
Bon voyage, bon appetit.

> One journeys still to inconvenient places,
> Rock-fast Kerry, fierce Kabul, Kashmir,
> Not because the going pleases
> Or the manners of the natives,
> To whom a long purse only makes the stranger dear.

> One accepts sharks to liven Achill's dullness,
> Flies, dung, dust in torpid Kandahar,
> Not because the mind is homeless
> Or the English landscape empty
> Of charm and strangeness seldom found afar.

> One endures din in Amber's silver temple,
> Goat beheaded by a sword on sand,
> Not because mystery is simpler
> Than doubt, and fear a veto
> To sharing common creeds of humankind.

> One journeys to those inconvenient places,
> Amber, Alexandroupolis, Achill,
> Not because the going pleases
> But lest the eye lack images
> To stir or calm the wild inconstant will.

# INDEX

187